The Good and Faithful Servant

A Small Group Study on Politics and Government for Christians

By

Hugh Hewitt

For Christians who vote, aware that
all over the world,
there are hundreds of millions of
their fellow believers
who never will be allowed to do so.

Table of Contents

Introduction ix

Week 1: "We Don't Want Nobody Nobody Sent" 17

Week 2: Six Commands 21

Week 3: "Garbage In, Garbage Out." Where Do You Get
Your Political Information From? 24

Week 4: Never Don't Talk About Politics and Religion 27

Week 5: What Do You Hear from Your Pulpit? 31

Week 6: Life Issues, Part 1: Does Abortion
Really Matter? 42

Week 7: Can Politics Feed the Hungry and Clothe the
Naked? 50

Week 8: National Security, Part 1: Is There Such a Thing
As A Just War? 55

Week 9: How Much Should the Rich Man Pay? 60

Week 10: What Does "Stewardship of the Earth" Mean? 66

Week 11: Do You Care About the Courts? 71

Week 12: Do We Need Borders? 76

Week 13: What About Illegal Immigrants? 79

Week 14: Should Christians Care About the Government's
Lack of Control on Pornography? 82

Week 15: Should the Government Punish Hateful
Speech?...85

Week 16: Should Same-Sex Marriage Be Allowed? 91

Week 17: Life Issues, Part 2: What About Stem Cell
Research?..96

Week 18: Life Issues, Part 3: Do We Care About
Euthanasia? 107

Week 19: National Security, Part 2: How Much Defense
Spending Is Enough?..120

Week 20: National Security, Part 3: Afghanistan, Iraq, Darfur
and Rwanda: When Should the U.S. Invade? 124

Week 21: National Security, Part 4: Does Christ Condemn
Waterboarding? 129

Week 22: The Problem of Race: Where to Now? 135

Week 23: The Islamists and the West: How Great
a Threat?..141

Week 24: How Urgent Are the Days (and Do You Act
Accordingly)? 147

Week 25: Do You Contribute Time, Talent, and Treasure to
Politics? 152

Week 26: Do You Have The Courage To Lead? Does Your
Pastor? Does Your Church?.......................................156

Introduction

At the outset, let me say that this study won't make much sense to you if you don't believe that Jesus Christ is Lord, is alive, and that His teachings are as they are recorded in the four gospels. I also presume that the reader believes that Scripture is God's Word, intended to be studied and followed to the best of our abilities. This is a study for Christians in the mainstream of Christianity—"mere Christians," C.S. Lewis called us. The theology in the book is of the mainstream sort, not controversial, but also not dumbed or watered-down. The book holds to certain obvious teachings of the Christian faith—the Nicene Creed, for example—and unremarkable-to-most assertions such as the belief that intimate sexuality is intended by God to be limited to a married man and woman, that it is wrong to murder or steal, etc. If you are a Buddhist, a Muslim, or an atheist, this is not the book for you. On the other hand, I believe most mainstream Catholics and Protestants will find little to object to in the theology I state, though perhaps much to argue with in its applications.

If you do believe that Christ is real, is risen, and cares deeply about the actions of every individual in His created order, read on.

According to ABC News' exit polling date for the 2008 presidential election, Barack Obama received millions of votes from dedicated Christians. President Obama received 45% of all Protestant votes and 54% of all Catholic votes. Of course, President Obama received an enormous outpouring of support from the African-American Christian community, but he did well among white Christians as well, with 34% of white Protestants and 47% of white Catholics pulling the lever for the new president. These include many weekly and more-than-weekly church attendees. 32% of all Protestants who attend church weekly voted for President Obama, and 49% of weekly mass-attending Catholics did so as well. (President Obama's numbers increased among self-described Protestants and Catholics who did not attend on at least a weekly basis, garnering 45% and 58% of these less-than-regular church-goers' votes respectively.)

Strikingly, President Obama won the votes of 24% of self-described "white evangelical/born-again Christians." The AP reported from its exit polling that "one in four voters were white born-again evangelical Christians," and there were a total of more than 125 million votes cast. That means more than 30 million evangelical Christians voted for President Obama, and that doesn't include African-American evangelicals.

President Obama is fairly described as the most liberal candidate for the presidency ever. Whether or not he governs from the center, the center-left, or the left portion of the American political spectrum will be revealed only after years have passed.

But we can say with certainty that millions and millions of evangelical Christians voted for President Obama despite the conflict between his announced views on issues like abortion and same-sex marriage and those of most leaders of mainstream evangelical churches. It is difficult to say what this means, or to chose among many multiple meanings, any number of which could be true for different millions of people.

Some deeply devout Christians may have decided that wholesale change in the United States was necessary despite the certainty that President Obama would appoint very pro-abortion rights justices to the U.S. Supreme Court. Others may have concluded that Christians simply have to step aside and allow civil authorities to marry same-sex couples while redoubling their own efforts to bring a different vision of sexual morality to everyone in the culture, not just gays and lesbians. Still others may have felt that hard times obliged them to vote their pocketbooks regardless of what changes an Obama Administration might bring when it came to the rights of the unborn or the free exercise of religion.

The only thing that can be said with certainty is that there is no certainty as to what the election of 2008 meant for the direction of Christianity in America. On the one hand, Pastor Rick Warren's much-watched and praised candidate forum on August 17, 2008, demonstrated that evangelicals, from their most visible leaders to their rank-and-file care deeply about politics and the course of the nation. On the other hand, there is deep confusion and often strident debate about what those evangelicals should care about.

Most visible among the liberal evangelicals is the Sojourners' Jim Wallis, whose many books and media appearances preach liberal politics. (For a quick taste of the Christian left, visit www.sojo.net.) Alongside Warren stands the traditional evangelical leaders like James Dobson of Focus on the Family and Albert Mohler, Jr., president of the Southern Baptist Theological Seminary in Louisville, Kentucky. There are dozens and dozens of high-profile evangelicals spread out across the political spectrum, each one of whom has decided sets of views on how a Christian ought to think, act, and vote.

It is apparent to me, as a center-right evangelical with deep roots in the Roman Catholic and Presbyterian traditions—yes, Catholics can be evangelical—that the American Church has failed to infuse its people with a sense of mission as to politics, and has failed in an even more basic mission of educating its people on the basic political issues of the day. Sadly, millions of churchgoing Christians didn't even bother to vote. And, as noted above, tens of millions of self-described evangelical Christians voted for Barack Obama, a vote which seems to me to be quite simply impossible for most faithful Christians to cast—*if they have studied the issues and their obligations as a citizen of this world and of the kingdom.*

Now that's a controversial statement, certain to elicit angry responses from Obama supporters who are themselves devout, but who for whatever reason do not believe that the issue of abortion or same-sex marriage or other key issues matter nearly as much as I think they do, or who have somehow reached a conclusion that voting for President Obama was a better way to reach the goals of more babies born or traditional marriage strengthened.

This isn't a study devoted to debating with these people. I just don't see the point right now, though when President Obama's re-election looms or the elections of presidents after that occur at their regular four-year intervals, such conversations are inevitable and to be welcomed. Indeed, one of the problems plaguing the American church is an increasing reticence about political discussion. But those discussions are not timely, nor are most Christians prepared to conduct them *in an informed manner.*

Before those debates about the pros and cons of future candidates occur, Christians ought to know what they believe and why they believe it. Christians ought first to have asked themselves what issues matter and how candidates ought to be evaluated with regard to those issues. They also ought to ask themselves how to assess a candidate based on his or her campaigning techniques, his or her candor, his or her past giving to charity and church, his or her past church attendance, and a whole host of other issues. But they really need to know how Christian belief impacts issues in the new millennium. Christians have to get smart about politics because the freedom of the church—in the U.S. and abroad—and thus the church's ability to spread the Good News of Christ depends on politics.

This is a study guide devoted to sharpening the skills a Christian brings to political debate and analysis. There are millions of "small groups" at work in the United States every week, gatherings of men, women, or couples who collect at the same time and place each week for fellowship and study. I have belonged to one or more such groups for more than 30 years, as has almost every serious Protestant believer I have known, and increasingly, many Catholic believers as well.

It is my hope that many of these groups, including those made up exclusively of Obama voters, will use this book for their next 26 meetings—a half-year of studies. I hope it is a short course in how to think about Christ, politics, and the call of Jesus to the responsible practice of citizenship. Each week is designed with a standard formula in mind, which should be pretty familiar to most group study participants. First, spend the inevitable ten or fifteen minutes chatting about the weather or travel plans. Then a leader asks for prayer requests, and an opening prayer ensures. Next, on the assumption that the readings provided have been read, the leader asks first for general reactions and then for answers to the questions provided in the "Commentary and Questions" section. Pray at the conclusion of the conversation. Repeat each week for twenty-six weeks.

If there is enough interest in this study, I will begin a website where comments on each week's study can be posted, and where relevant links will be provided on an ongoing basis so that the weekly subjects can be continually updated with the most recent information relevant to the topics and the conversations. One of the key ingredients to being a responsible citizen and thus a faithful Christian is accurate, up-to-date information. The facts of this world, however uncomfortable, have to be the backbone of any discussion of a Christian's duties as a citizen. Uninformed or misinformed people don't just not contribute to a conversation; they hurt them by dealing in bad facts or illogical arguments. Participatory websites have lots of problems with "bad-faith" posters, mischief-makers, and the simply deranged, but if there is a large enough audience, the software can be designed to register users and thus limit the distractions from the malevolent-minded. Check in at HughHewitt.com to see if such a new site is launched.

The facts presented in each of these chapters are just that: facts. Of course there are billions of other facts not included that are relevant to the discussions herein, but if the conversation is about a Christian's duty vis-à-vis global warming, there are some obvious facts that need to be on the table before any conversation begins, and a spectrum of opinions about those facts that needs to be fairly conveyed. I have done my best to do this. Those who disagree can post at the website if it gets going. Responsible comments will be welcome, but polemic or simple virtual shouting will be deleted.

By way of background, I am at the time of this writing fifty-three. I have been a Christian since a very early age, always in a mixed Catholic-Presbyterian family, meaning I have been in either a Roman Catholic or Presbyterian church almost every weekend since 1956. I write from the perspective of a mere Christian, not a theologian. I believe Jesus Christ is God, is alive, is going to return and restore creation, and is the sole means of eternal salvation. Though I remain a noncombatant in the specifics of how that works, trusting that sincere, visible, and vocal faith in Christ is the key to happiness on this earth and in eternal life. I am a conservative Republican and have been since high school. I have written at length about politics in ten previous books, in hundreds of columns, and daily at my blog, www.HughHewitt.com. I am in my twentieth year as a broadcast journalist, a career which included a decade on television and which, for the last ten years, has been anchored in my weekday nationally syndicated radio show. I am a professor at Chapman University Law School and have been since it opened its doors in 1994. My undergraduate degree is in government from Harvard College and my law school degree is from the University of Michigan Law School. I served six years in the Reagan Administration in a variety of posts, including Assistant Counsel in the White House and Special Assistant to two Attorneys General. My last job in D.C. was as Deputy Director of the U.S. Office of Personnel Management, which followed unanimous confirmation by the Senate of the United States. Since returning to California with my wonderful wife of twenty-six years, I have served on the California Arts Council, the South Coast Air Quality Management District, and for a decade, on Orange County's Children and Families Commission, which annually spends about $40 million in cigarette tax revenue. I tell you all this to convey that I really do think about and study politics and government, and that I consider public service a noble calling and teaching a spiritual gift.

I am married, in the twenty-eighth year of a wonderful partnership. Our three children are grown, and we love them dearly and are very proud of them, but years of parenting have also colored my views on many of the issues discussed herein. I write form the perspective of one who worries about how the world will look for any grandchildren we may be blessed with down the road. To be middle-aged and an empty-nester, but not yet so old as to have retired, is perhaps the best vantage point from which to consider the big issues: You can combine knowledge with experience yet not be indifferent to the massive amount of change you know you will have to cope with in the years ahead. My gramps, A.T. Rohl, lived to just shy of one hundred and two. I have a keen interest in the next few decades if for no other reason than my genes may require me to live through them.

Please feel free to send me your questions and comments via e-mail at hugh@hughewitt.com. Of all the books I have written in the past, *The War Against the West* might be of the most use in this study, collecting as it does in one place most of my interviews with experts on the war against Islamist terrorism, which I think has to drive a great deal of politics in America for the foreseeable future. Younger men and women might also value *In, But Not Of: A Guide to Christian Ambition*, which is also available in paperback under the simple title *A Guide To Christian Ambition*. These books are available via my website.

I think you are in for a challenging twenty-six meetings if you undertake this study, so I close the introduction with this caution: Political argument should never sunder Christian fellowship, even when the arguments are sharp and necessarily so because of the importance of the issues. My closest friend, the godfather of one of my children, is a lifelong Democrat who served in very senior positions in the Clinton White House and is a confidante and advisor still to the liberal elites of Washington, D.C. He's a wonderful, wonderful man who happens to be wrong on most issues. I am working on him as he has been working on me since we roomed together at Harvard thirty years ago. It is that spirit of debate and genuine exchange that I hope infuses your conversations in the weeks ahead.

Week 1:
"We Don't Want Nobody Nobody Sent"

Scripture:

My son, hear the instruction of your father, And do not forsake the law of your mother.

—Proverbs 1:8:

Children, obey your parents in all things, for this is well pleasing to the Lord.

—Colossians 3:20

Readings:

A strong case could be made for theocracy, American-style, if the word were defined not in the conventional way but according to its root meaning. Democracy signifies the rule of the demos, the people. Strictly speaking, theocracy means the rule not of churches or priests but of theos, God. It won't do to deny that many conservatives, even while unambiguously affirming the traditional American separation of church and state, would add more theos to the democratic mix than is currently the case. I choose not to call myself a theocrat because I know how eager liberal secularists would be to twist the word against me. Dishonestly they would make it appear that I wish to impose a literal biblical theocracy, that I would dumbly imitate word for word the political structure of king, priesthood, and religious high court that existed in biblical antiquity. "Yet, in a subtler sense, are we not all theocrats now?"

—David Klinghoffer

To anyone who takes God seriously, every election poses a radical question. Will we vote with Him, or against Him? The Bible is an unapologetically political book and an extremely conservative one. Some political views offend God, and those views are mostly liberal. To misperceive Scripture's political meaning is as much an error as to misperceive its moral meaning.

Yet liberal leaders and left-wing activists have obscured these clear truths. One thinks of Senator Hillary Clinton, who in a June 2007 forum on CNN claimed that it was her Christian beliefs that underlie her stands on controversial issues. With reference to herself and her fellow Democratic candidates, Clinton forthrightly said, "I think you can sense how we are attempting to try to inject faith into policy." That line alone, spoken by a Republican, would have been trumpeted on the front page of countless newspapers and Web sites as proof that the speaker harbors a secret plot to turn America into a theocracy along the lines of Iran or Saudi Arabia. Even a forthrightly Christian candidate like Mike Huckabee feels he has to be more cautious with his rhetoric than any Democrat does.

—David Klinghoffer

Be more concerned with your character than with your reputation. Your character is what you really are while your reputation is merely what others think you are.

—John Wooden

Decades ago, when the machine was far stronger, young Abner Mikva, an Obama mentor who served as a congressman, federal judge and counsel, tried to volunteer at the 8th Ward Regular Democratic headquarters. "We don't want nobody nobody sent," the party operative told him. When Mikva said he was from the University of Chicago and was willing to work free, the man said, "We don't want nobody from the University of Chicago in this organization."

—Peter Slevin

Commentary and Questions:

Abner Mikva was a judge of the United States Court of Appeals for the District of Columbia Circuit the year I clerked on the court for Judges Roger Robb and George MacKinnon. True to what one would expect from a former Chicago congressman, Judge Mikva was a warm, colorful, and very talkative judge, and the story recounted above of Mikva's first effort to dive into politics is pure Mikva.

It is also pure politics, and not just of the Chicago-machine variety. Almost all politics is simply a contest between competing organizations composed of people who know each other to some degree for the affections and support of people who don't know any of the competing groups at all.

Politics is mostly about group identity and the collective desires of those groups, which have been called "voting blocs" for as long as I can recall. The Irish-Catholics, black voters, gay and lesbian voters, soccer moms, blue collar workers, Reagan Democrats—these and scores of other tags are shorthand descriptions of loosely aligned groups of voters who generally pull the lever for the same candidates and causes on the basis of perceived shared self-interests.

Much of this study depends upon understanding why when Christians go to vote they ought to identify themselves as Christians first, and why they ought to analyze the issues and candidates from their Christian worldview. To get to that posture, though, it is important to begin with the self-knowledge of where you have been as a citizen.

So who are you, politically speaking? Who have you voted for? Whom did your parents vote for? What makes you think the way you do when it comes to politics and elections? Who influenced you?

Spend this week's meeting on your family's history. Each member of the group should give a few minute brief on their political history, beginning with the politics of their grandparents and then their parents, whether or not politics was a subject of much discussion around the dinner table. Much of political identity is simply inherited—a quiet passing of attitudes and assumptions from generation to generation. This is one reason why political change is often so slow to occur. When a decisive declaration of political beliefs occurs and is lived out by a father and a mother over many years, most children will absorb the lessons the parents teach, whether those lessons are explicit or simply transmitted with looks and grunts.

So where did you come from? Who sent you? In a couple of weeks we will look at your personal political journey, but this week, focus on what you started with as your inheritance. And would your parents be surprised at the way you vote today and the issues that matter most to you?

Week 2:
Six Commands

Scripture:

And what does the Lord require of you? To do justice, love mercy, and walk humbly with your God.

—Micah 6:8

"Love the Lord your God with all your heart and with all your soul and with all your mind." This is the first and greatest commandment. And the second is like it: "Love your neighbor as yourself." All the Law and the Prophets hang on these two commandments.

—Matthew 22: 37-39

Render unto Caesar what is Caesar's, and to God what is God's.

—Matthew 22: 21

Readings:

The hope of a secure and livable world lies with disciplined nonconformists who are dedicated to justice, peace and brotherhood.

—Martin Luther King, Jr.

Commentary and Questions:

The selections from Scripture are among the most familiar of verses to anyone who has attended church on even a semi-regular basis over a few years. They are also favorites of Christian writers wrestling with the questions connected to how a Christian ought to shape his or her responses to political events. They can be used to justify pretty much any position, by the way, but that doesn't render them useless.

Justice. Kindness. Humility. Obedience to the laws. These are the values embedded in these lines, and no Christian should be able to survey their political participation and allegiances without being able to conclude easily that their past actions conform to these goals.

"What is 'justice'?" is a question that human philosophers have been struggling with since they began the quest for wisdom. But in the passage from Micah, God assumes that His audience knows exactly what it means, and more often than not, we do. It means fairness and right decision-making. Justice is easiest to see where it is absent, as in a tyranny. We know, for example, that Saddam Hussein's Iraq—like Hitler's Germany, Stalin's Soviet Union, and Pol Pot's Cambodia—was a profoundly unjust place. We know that today Mugabe's Zimbabwe, the Darfur in Sudan, and Kim Jong-il's North Korea are also thoroughly unjust and monstrous regimes.

We can say with certainty about all these regimes past and present that large numbers of innocent people were imprisoned and killed by despots. Cruelty is a mark of injustice. We also should be able to easily recognize that any nation that is governed by the rule of law is a nation attempting to be just, even if it fails sometimes. Similarly, we know what kindness and love are. No lectures needed here. We also know that the humility necessary to "walk humbly with God" will be reflected in a humility with others in all aspects of life.

This means our politics, while energetic and played to win, must not become indifferent to the participants opposite us on any given issue or in any given election. The humility we should all bring to politics doesn't mean silence or even deference, only the recognition that on any given issue or on many issues we might be horribly, terribly wrong. Even the greatest of our political leaders, like Lincoln and FDR, were often horribly, terribly wrong. Lincoln couldn't chose a successful commander for the Army of the Potomac until he had run through McClellen and many others before settling on Grant. FDR never did solve the Great Depression—World War II's demands for industrial output solved it for him.

Obedience means the obvious as well: Know and obey the laws. Pay your taxes. And perform the duties of a citizen. This last part should catch up those Christians who do not vote. Caesar didn't require much of his subjects in the time of Jesus other than obedience, especially with regards to taxes. But in the United States in the twenty-first century, much more is required, including an informed and active citizenry.

So the questions of the week are as obvious and as fundamental as the readings: Do you think the U.S. is a just country? More or less just than European countries? More or less just than, say, Cuba and the People's Republic of China? Why or why not? Do you conduct your political participation to the extent that you are involved, with kindness toward opponents and humility about the prospect that you might be wrong? Have you been wrong—not in the sense of predicting wrongly on who might win, but about a central proposition of your political views? And finally, how's your participation level? Have you voted in every election for which you have been eligible? If not, why not? And did you consider not voting to be sinful?

More on that next week.

Week 3:
"Garbage In, Garbage Out."
Where Do You Get Your Political
Information From?

Scripture:

Do not be deceived: "Evil company corrupts good habits."

—Corinthians 15:33

Readings:

You know you are being influenced when you say, "I might have written that myself if I'd only had a little more time."

—E.M. Foster

All great change in America begins at the dinner table.

—Ronald Reagan

When the conduct of men is designed to be influenced, persuasion, kind unassuming persuasion, should ever be adopted. It is an old and true maxim that "a drop of honey catches more flies than a gallon of gall." So with men. If you would win a man to your cause, first convince him that you are his sincere friend. Therein is a drop of honey that catches his heart, which, say what he will, is the great highroad to his reason, and which, once gained, you will find but little trouble in convincing him of the justice of your cause, if indeed that cause is really a good one.

—Abraham Lincoln

Our children are our only hope for the future, but we are their only hope for their present and their future.

—Zig Zigler

Commentary and Questions:

"Who are you going with?"

This is one of the most common questions directed from parents to teenagers, or at least it ought to be. Parents know that the choice of company is usually the greatest determinant of the sort of behavior the kids will be up to. The company he or she keeps will greatly define the choices he or she makes. The company you keep also determines the choices you make, though it is often less obvious as we live through our adult years. Sometimes even our company is only vaguely understood to be company.

If, as a young man or woman, you choose to run with a fast crowd, expect to find yourself in places that would shock your Sunday school teachers. If, as an old man or woman, you live among those who rarely move from the sofa, you will quickly become as sedate as your neighbors. Live with an active community of peers, however, and you will be a vital, active senior.

These are obvious truths because we know we take on the traits of the community in which we live and spend the most time. This is human nature, and it isn't going to change soon. So from whom are you taking your political cues? Look around the table. Before you began this study, did this group ever talk politics? Does your church sponsor political discussions and debates? Do you find that most of your pastor's or priest's sermons deal with politics?

If you are a typical Christian, the answers to the last three questions will be "No, we don't talk politics in small group," "No, my church doesn't sponsor political discussions or debates," and "No, my pastor doesn't talk much from the pulpit about politics." Which leads us back to the first question: From where do you get your opinions and information on things political?

Next week's study will deal with much greater specificity about information flows and a church's role when it comes to politics, but today is just a discussion of roots: How did you come to hold the opinions you have?

For many Americans, politics is part of the family inheritance. If you are an Irish-Catholic in Boston, chances are you are a Democrat. If, as Tim Russert described in his wonderful memoir of his life growing up in Buffalo, your dad is a garbage man and the nuns at your school all were thrilled with the election of Jack Kennedy, it isn't very likely that you are going to end up as a Republican.

If, on the other hand, you grew up at the county club and your dad included denunciations of Democrats' tax policy over every Sunday dinner, chances are you headed out in life leaning GOP (unless you came of age during the Vietnam War—a very special case.)

To set the stage for all that follows, review quickly what you covered two weeks ago—the family political history—and then ask yourselves and each other why you are where you are on the political spectrum today. Were you born into the political party you still inhabit, or did you make a big jump at some point? And regardless of the details of your story, how much of your political make-up has been because of who you are and where and with whom you have lived as opposed to what you have read or studied?

Next week we look at where your political information is coming from. This week, try and figure out where you are coming from.

Week 4:
Never Don't Talk About Politics and Religion

Scripture:

Then the Pharisees went and plotted how they might entangle Him in His talk. And they sent to Him their disciples with the Herodians, saying, "Teacher, we know that You are true, and teach the way of God in truth; nor do You care about anyone, for You do not regard the person of men. Tell us, therefore, what do You think? Is it lawful to pay taxes to Caesar, or not?" But Jesus perceived their wickedness, and said, "Why do you test Me, you hypocrites? Show Me the tax money." So they brought Him a denarius. And He said to them, "Whose image and inscription is this?" They said to Him, "Caesar's." And He said to them, "Render therefore to Caesar the things that are Caesar's, and to God the things that are God's." When they had heard these words, they marveled, and left Him and went their way.

—Matthew 22:15-22

Readings:

We have no government armed with power capable of contending with human passions unbridled by morality and religion. Avarice, ambition, revenge or gallantry would break the strongest cords of our Constitution as a whale goes through a net. Our Constitution is designed only for a moral and religious people. It is wholly inadequate for any other.

—John Adams

For the first time in a long while, then, there is a serious rethinking of the politics of Jesus in America—or at least the efforts of different elements in the country, from believers of progressive, moderate and conservative bents, to claim they are acting in his name in the public sphere. "In this world ye shall have tribulation," Jesus told his disciples—a decided understatement. Though he added the reassurance that they should "be of good cheer; I have overcome the world," those disciples and their heirs down two millennia still face tribulation and trouble, and currently stand at a crossroads. Can they move beyond the apparent confines of the religious right as popularly understood, or are they destined to seem harsh and intolerant—the opposite of what their own faith would have them be? The search for an answer to that question goes to the heart of what American life and politics will look like as we face a landmark midterm election this week and a wide-open presidential race two years hence.

—Newsweek, November 2006

I long for the day when the precepts of the Christian religion shall be the rule among all classes of men, in all transactions. I often hear it said, "Do not bring religion into politics." This is precisely where it ought to be brought, and set there in the face of all men as on a candlestick.

—Charles Spurgeon

Commentary and Questions:

Because I have to talk about politics and government a good part of most weekdays for my three-hour radio show, it is my business to stay informed about what is going on in the world. Because I interview authors fairly frequently, I read a lot of books about current events. Because I appear on other radio and television shows, I study up on the subjects assigned. Because I have to post to my blog at HughHewitt.com every day, I spend most mornings reading and commenting on newspapers.

Even before I got into journalism twenty years ago, and into government a decade earlier, I loved politics and public policy. I studied it as an undergrad. I even read political magazines as a high school student. This is far from the norm in America, though also far from unusual. Some of us love politics the way others love sports. Some, like me, love both—and some neither.

But the hard fact about democracy is that citizens get to vote no matter how much or little they know about politics and government, and I wouldn't have it any other way. For a democratic republic to endure, citizens must care about how the government is functioning, even if many of them have no idea about the issues of the day and even if many of them are objectively ill-informed on any particular issue. It would be better if far more people knew far much more about the debates raging inside of Congress or knew the names of the members of the cabinet or the size of the military or the extent of the government's debt. But generally, they don't. In fact, most people reading this book and participating in this study won't be up to speed on most of the issues covered herein over the next five months. You haven't got the time to begin with, and when you get home from work, the last thing you want to do is watch a C-SPAN debate on the trade deficit.

How about you? What's your personal intake of political information? Do you read a newspaper daily? Read any political magazines? Listen to talk radio or watch O'Reilly or Chris Matthews? Do you think you are an average American when it comes to seeking out political information?

The next twenty-two times you will be getting together will involve conversations about political events from a Christian worldview. Are you prepared for those conversations or are you coming at this from a long period of indifference?

Here's the topic for this week: Spell out for your friends how you stay informed. Many of you simply won't be in the habit of doing much in the way of reading or listening to political talk, which is fine, but be candid about that and explain to your friends in the study why. Then ask whether the country can prosper if the voters are generally not very interested in political debate and current events involving the government. Finally, compare the effort you put into learning about your faith—church attendance, Bible study or related reading, small group participation, etc.—with the amount of effort you put into being a citizen. Is the energy you devote to the one more or less the same as the other, or does your faith get far more attention than your politics? If there is an imbalance, does that make sense when the freedom to practice your faith depends upon maintaining a government that protects freedom of religion?

Week 5:
What Do You Hear from Your Pulpit?

Scripture:

And He Himself gave some to be apostles, some prophets, some evangelists, and some pastors and teachers, for the equipping of the saints for the work of ministry, for the edifying of the body of Christ.

—Ephesians 4:11, 12

Readings:

The basis for the Christian worldview, of course, is God's revelation in Scripture. Yet sadly, many believers fail to understand that Scripture is intended to be the basis for all of life. In the past centuries, the secular world asserted a dichotomy between science and religion, between fact and value, between objective knowledge and subjective feeling. As a result, Christians often think in terms of the same false dichotomy, allowing our belief system to be reduced to little more than private feelings and experience, completely divorced from objective facts.

—Chuck Colson

And when they said the Church ought to give us the lead, they ought to mean that some Christians—those who have the right talents,—should be economists and statesmen... and that their whole efforts in politics and economics should be directed to putting... (the Golden Rule) into action.... The application of Christian principles to say trade unionism or education must come from Christian trade unionists and Christian schoolmasters; just as Christian literature comes from Christian novelists and dramatists and not from the bench of Bishops getting together and trying to write plays and novels in their spare time.

—C.S. Lewis

Commentary and Questions:

I have never been a fan of mixing the pulpit with politics. A few years ago I even wrote in a book for young people that counseled that they should consider the callings of politician and pastor to be wholly separate because the mixing of the two led to very bad results for both. When I wrote that, I specifically referenced Dr. Jerry Falwell. Though I admired Dr. Falwell's faith, great-heartedness, and good humor, I thought that he had done more harm than good to conservative politics over the years because he was too big a target.

While I continue to believe that evangelical leaders who enter into political debates should not be ordained clergy, I am also more and more convinced that the church in America has fallen down on the job of instructing its people on the importance of informed participation in a democracy. In early 2009, I asked a Biola University theology professor, Dr. J.P. Moreland, to discuss with me on air the role of the church in the new age of politics under President Obama. Here are the relevant portions of that conversation:

HH: J.P. Moreland is a prolific author and many of you know his work. He's a professor of philosophy at the Biola University at the Talbott School of Theology there, and his most recent book is *The God Question: An Invitation to a Life of Meaning.* J.P. Moreland, welcome to *The Hugh Hewitt Show.*

JPM: It's great to be with you, Hugh.

HH: Thanks for joining me, J.P. The point of this series of conversations is to reorient people who are a little bit confused, I guess that's right. What do you see in the reaction among evangelicals as President Obama takes power?

JPM: Well, I think evangelicals have failed to develop a political philosophy that's holistic. I think instead, they've tended to be issue-based rather than having an entire approach to government. And so I have a lot of concerns as an evangelical about the Obama presidency precisely because I'm a Christian evangelical.

HH: What kind of concerns?

JPM: Well, the first, as a Christian, the first thing that I see can be understood by the difference between negative and positive rights. A negative right is a right for me to be protected from harm if I try to get something for myself. A positive right would be my right to have something provided for me. If healthcare is a negative right, then the state has an obligation to keep people from preventing me from getting health care and discriminating against me. If healthcare's a positive right, then the state has an obligation to provide it for me. As I read the New Testament, the government's responsibility—and by the way, I think the Old Testament prophets say this, too—is [that] the government's job is to protect negative rights, not to provide positive rights. So as a Christian, I believe in a minimal government. It's not the government's job to be providing the healthcare benefits for people. So I will be looking to see if Obama does things to minimize the role of government in culture, and to provide for as much human freedom as possible.

33

HH: Now we'll go down a couple of issues after the break, but I'd like to begin, because a lot of pastors look to you, J.P. Moreland. They've been reading your work for years, you're out there in the churches throughout the United States giving seminars, et cetera: What kind of role do they have going forward? Obviously, a lot of them are very leery about touching on politics in the pulpit. What do you expect of pastors in this new age?

JPM: Well, I think they've got to do the opposite. I think that Christians believe the Bible has something to say about everything. The Bible has something to say about science, it has something to say about sex in marriage, it has something to say about money. Well, why wouldn't the Bible has something to say about the state? It doesn't make any sense to me that the Bible would be silent about this one topic when it has something to say about virtually everything else, including art, history, and so on. So I think what pastors have to do is to simply teach their congregations and lead by example about what the Bible says about the role of the state in public life. I think it's more important to teach a general political theology than it is to get involved in specific issues from the beginning, because it's going to be your political philosophy that informs those issues. And so if I were a pastor, I would begin to develop a theology about what the Bible says about the role of the state.

HH: And that's where we started this conversation. Obviously, you started from that first principle of negative/positive rights. But if you're just a pastor out there, or you're someone who wants to go to their pastor and say, "You know, we really, we blew it, we didn't get involved in politics, we didn't take a stand on anything, and now we're in the most left-leaning moment in American history," would you agree with that, J.P?

JPM: I would absolutely agree with it, and I think that we have to understand today, and this is something that pastors need to understand, that to be left-leaning in these days means to be secular. And so one concern that the Christian Church will have towards the movement of politics to the far left is that this represents the secularization of American culture, and the minimalization of religious ideas. You know, Richard John Neuhaus made the point that once religion is taken out of the public square, the state will become totalitarian.... And I think pastors have a responsibility to teach about a whole range of issues from a Christian perspective. Let me give you another example, Hugh. As I understand that love and compassion have to be voluntary, you can't force someone to show compassion to someone, but the state does its job by coercion in taxes, and it forces money in one direction as opposed to another. It follows from this that the state can't show compassion. The state can mete out justice, but it cannot show compassion if compassion is in fact voluntary. It would seem to me, then, as a Christian view of the state, that it is not the state's job by and large to be showing compassion, but rather to be enforcing criminal justice and so on. If I were a pastor then, I would be emphasizing the fact that it is primarily charities' job to show compassion, not the state's.

HH: I think the evangelical movement has hit the rocks. I think they don't know what to do politically, and I think that there are a lot of people who are wondering what to do politically. And in a very practical sense, I think there are a lot of pastors and a lot of lay leadership wondering what should we do. In a very practical way, what's your recommendation to a pastor who thinks that, okay, the country's gone very far to the left, or to his lay board that thinks he needs to step up and get involved without endorsing people from the pulpit, which is verboten under the tax code?

JPM: Sure.

HH: What practical steps do you advise?

JPM: First practical step is that we simply have got to realize that we must mobilize our people to vote. Being involved in politics is not unChristian. In fact, it's a part of our calling as Christians. Why? Because we are supposed to do good to all people, including the household of faith. And to do good to all people means establishing just laws and a just and a stable social order. And that's the job of the state. It's political. So the first thing a pastor should do and the church should do is to enlist people like the dickens to be involved in the political process and vote. It is unconscionable that we have these rights, and that we have an obligation as disciples of Jesus to try to bring goodness and truth to society, that we don't use all means available to promote just laws and a just and stable social order through the political process. And so voting is absolutely critical. That's step one.

HH: Would you recommend pastors preach from the pulpit on the necessity of registering to vote?

JPM: Oh, there's no question about it. Absolutely. In fact, it's a derelict of duty if a pastor does not, in a free society like ours, where we have an opportunity to be a part of promoting a just society and a good, stable social order with regard to laws and politics, [does] not encourage from the pulpit that people become informed on these issues, vote, and so on. Absolutely.

HH: All right, step two?

JPM: Step two, there should be teaching about four topics—first, the culture of life. It is important to vote for a political party that seeks to promote a culture of life. That's a Christian value. Second, we ought to be promoting a minimal view of the government that follows from my distinction about negative and positive rights. The government has a very limited role in culture as far as the New Testament is concerned. Third, we ought to promote a government that seeks to maintain control over crime and has a strong anti-crime policy. And then finally, it is primarily the job of charity and the local church to care for the poor, and to be involved in that kind of outreach. It is not primarily the state's job. And so what a pastor should be doing is teaching and leading by example in his church about reaching out to the poor, providing education, food, clothing and job training, and doing it through charities rather than the coercive machinery of the state.

HH: Now J.P. Moreland, if there's a liberal driving around, and I know there are, there are hundreds of thousands of them, actually, driving around and listening to you, and I hope they read your book, *The God Question*—they are saying, "But that's a recipe for having evangelical pastors endorsing the Republican Party."

JPM: Well, if the Republican Party is closer to a Christian view, then so be it. If the Democratic Party's closer, then so be it. I'm a Republican at this point because I find that its policies, when Republicans are acting like Republicans, tend to be closer to my read of the Old and New Testaments than the Democratic Party. So I don't vote Republican because I care about Republicans, or because I'm politically conservative for its own sake. I'm political conservative because I think that's the view that the Old and New Testaments teach, and I've done a fair amount of study about this. Now I could be wrong, but that's my conviction. And I think I've read the Scriptures fairly clearly on these questions.

HH: Do you think pastors will get into trouble? I mean, they're all going to say to you, "That's very nice, but I'm going to have my Democrats leave, and they're going to take their contributions with them, and then they're going to call the IRS and I'm going to get audited. And I just as soon talk about the Beatitudes, and not connect them up to voting."

JPM: Well, if you keep doing that, then what you're creating is a secular-sacred split in the lives of your parishioners. They can allow Jesus Christ to have some-thing to say about their private spiritual lives, but Jesus Christ is not allowed to say anything when it comes to their public life. I find that kind of discipleship to be completely unacceptable. If, as a Christian, and those who are listening aren't Christians need to understand that those of us who are Christians want to seek to follow Jesus as best we can with all our flaws and all of our problems, but that's our goal. It would follow, then, that we should want to follow Jesus throughout all of life, including life as citizens of the state if the New Testament and Old Testament teach on that, and they do.

HH: Is it malpractice, J.P. Moreland, for an evangelical pastor to be silent on such things?

JPM: Well, absolutely. I mean, how could a pastor refrain from teaching what the Bible has to say about the important issues of our day that his or her parishioners have got to face? The Bible is not silent on these matters. I say again, Hugh, Christians believe the Bible has something to say about science and religion. Christians believe the Bible has something to say about abortion and euthanasia, about economics, about money, about marriage. Why all of a sudden do we think the Bible doesn't have anything at all to say about the state and the political life? Why that just makes no sense whatsoever. The problem is not that the Bible doesn't teach about these things, the problem is that the church is illiterate because there's been a lack of teaching on it.

HH: This is not a religious program. This is a secular program. But the evangelicals have been routed. They've been absolutely destroyed at the polls, and they're sitting there on the sidelines wondering what happened, where did we go wrong, why is this government so far left? And, J.P., how urgent are the times? And how urgent the repair of the evangelical project in politics?

JPM: It's extremely urgent, Hugh, for precisely the reason that you signaled. Evangelicals have withdrawn, they have been routed as you pointed out, and the culture is moving rapidly toward Europe. It's becoming increasingly secularized. And anyone who's concerned about the secularization of culture should be concerned that a major portion of the population, the evangelical vote, be increasingly articulate and understand what it believes and why in this arena.

HH: And do you see hopeful signs in that regard?

JPM: I do see hopeful signs, because I think more and more Christians are tired of having Jesus Christ simply be a private part of their lives, and they want to be involved in the public arena. I will say there's one important link to this whole thing that I haven't mentioned yet, and that is that the key to an evangelical political involvement is what is called natural moral law. Natural moral law is the belief that there is objective morality that can be known by all people from creation, without the Bible. Natural moral law teaches that there is a right and wrong in the created world that can be known by people without having to turn to the Bible. This is important because the evangelical does not want to place the state under Scripture. That would be to create a theocracy, and that has never been a good idea. What we want is we want to place the state under the natural moral law. Therefore, if an evangelical is going to be for traditional marriage, and it's going to be against gay marriage, it cannot use Scripture to argue that case in the public square. It can be preached from the pulpit that this is a biblical view, but when it comes to political engagement, it is not our attempt to place the state under the Bible, but to place it under the natural moral law. So it would follow, then, that Christians need to learn how to provide independent arguments for traditional marriage that do not require premises from the Scriptures.

HH: And on any other issue as well.

JPM: Say it again?

HH: And on any other issue.

JPM: Oh, yeah, I was just using that to illustrate, absolutely on any other issue. So it's perfectly legitimate for pastors to teach what the Bible teaches about a range of issues, but if we're going to be involved in a pluralistic culture, we want to bring the state under the objective natural moral law rather than bring it under Scripture because we do not want to create a theocracy.

Do you agree with Dr. Moreland's views on how a church should be approaching political involvement and debate about political issues? If so, is your church and your pastor measuring up to that mark? Is it part of your job to change your church's approach to politics, and if so, how might you go about that?

Week 6:
Life Issues, Part 1:
Does Abortion Really Matter?

Scripture:

> You shall not murder.
>
> —Exodus 20:13

> Cursed is he who accepts a bribe to strike down an innocent person.
>
> —Deuteronomy 27:25a

> There are six things which the LORD hates, yes, seven which are an abomination to Him: haughty eyes, a lying tongue, and hands that shed innocent blood...
>
> —Proverbs 6:16-19

> For behold, when the sound of your greeting reached my ears, the baby leaped in my womb for joy.
>
> —Luke 1:44

> If men struggle with each other and strike a woman with child so that she gives birth prematurely...
>
> —Exodus 21:22

> For You formed my inward parts; You wove me in my mother's womb. I will give thanks to You, for I am fearfully and wonderfully made; wonderful are Your works, and my soul knows it very well. My frame was not hidden from You, when I was made in secret, and skillfully wrought in the depths of the earth; Your eyes have seen my unformed substance; and in Your book

were all written the days that were ordained for me, when as yet there was not one of them.

—Psalm 139:13-16

For he will be great in the sight of the Lord; and he will drink no wine or liquor, and he will be filled with the Holy Spirit while yet in his mother's womb.

—Luke 1:15.

Before I formed you in the womb I knew you, and before you were born I consecrated you.

—Jeremiah. 1:5

Then he called for Solomon his son and charged him to build a house for the LORD, the God of Israel. David said to Solomon, "My son, I had it in my heart to build a house to the name of the LORD my God. But the word of the LORD came to me, saying, 'You have shed much blood and have waged great wars. You shall not build a house to my name, because you have shed so much blood before me on the earth.'"

—1 Chronicles 22:6-8 (ESV)

On you was I cast from my birth, and from my mother's womb you have been my God.

—Psalm 22:10-11 (ESV)

Blessed are those who wash their robes, so that they may have the right to the tree of life and that they may enter the city by the gates. Outside are the dogs and sorcerers and the sexually immoral and murderers and idolaters, and everyone who loves and practices falsehood.

—Revelation 22:14-15 (ESV)

They sacrificed their sons and their daughters to the demons; they poured out innocent blood, the blood of their sons and daughters, whom they sacrificed to the idols of Canaan, and the land was polluted with blood.

—Psalm 106:37-38 (ESV)

And they burned their sons and their daughters as offerings and used divination and omens and sold themselves to do evil in the sight of the LORD, provoking him to anger. Therefore the LORD was very angry with Israel and removed them out of his sight.

—2 Kings 17:17-18 (ESV)

When you spread out your hands, I will hide my eyes from you; even though you make many prayers, will not listen; your hands are full of blood. Wash yourselves; make yourselves clean; remove the evil of your deeds from before my eyes; cease to do evil, learn to do good; seek justice, correct oppression; bring justice to the fatherless, plead the widow's cause.

—Isaiah 1:13-17 (ESV)

For this is the message that you have heard from the beginning, that we should love one another. We should not be like Cain, who was of the evil one and murdered his brother.

—1 John 3:11-12 (ESV)

Readings:

You don't have to be a constitutional scholar to know that reading a so-called "right to abortion" into any of our nation's founding documents is a gross deviation from the intent of our Founding Fathers. An honest and accurate reading of our Constitution simply does not allow for it. Yet pro-abortion forces, from 1973 straight through to today, have always argued that legalized abortion somehow results in better lives for women. But the facts tell a very different story. What many have touted as the ultimate expression of "women's rights" has actually victimized women to an unprecedented degree.

—Dr. James Dobson

ABORTION STATISTICS, WORLDWIDE:

Number of abortions per year: Approximately 46 million

Number of abortions per day: Approximately 126,000

About 26 million women obtain legal abortions each year, while an additional 20 million abortions are obtained in countries where it is restricted or prohibited by law.

Worldwide, the lifetime average is about 1 abortion per woman.

ABORTION STATISTICS, UNITED STATES:

Number of abortions in 2005: 1.21 million

From 1973 through 2008 almost 50 million legal abortions occurred in the U.S.

To accept the fact that after fertilization has taken place a new human has come into being is no longer a matter of taste or opinion… it is plain experimental evidence.

—Dr. Jerome LeJeune

It is scientifically correct to say that an individual human life begins at conception.

—Prof. Micheline Matthews-Roth

By all the criteria of modern molecular biology, life is present from the moment of conception.

—Dr. Hymie Gordon

I have learned from my earliest medical education that human life begins at the time of conception…. I submit that human life is present throughout this entire sequence from conception to adulthood and that any interruption at any point throughout this time constitutes a termination of human life….

—Dr. Alfred Bongioanni

Commentary and Questions:

Is there any issue that most people want to talk less about than abortion? Though pro-life activists are very, very visible exceptions to this rule, the rule most definitely is that polite company does not discuss abortion. Not even talk radio discusses abortion much, so unpleasant is the discussion.

The reasons behind this reticence are many and mostly obvious. First, the subject matter is gruesome, especially as it inevitably must deal with unborn children aborted late in a woman's pregnancy. Next, after nearly 50 million abortions in the United States since 1973, the number of women who have experienced the procedure is in the millions as well, and they are going to react very emotionally to the subject as it involves judgment about their own past acts in a way that discussions about almost any other issue do not. (Most issues dealing with sexuality become highly charged quickly because of the widespread personal experience with such issues. Debates about defense spending or off-shore oil exploration, by contrast, are highly removed from an individual's own actions and are thus unlikely to trigger defensiveness or embarrassment.) Third, any thoroughgoing discussion about abortion has to bring up some very difficult issues relating to rape, incest, and very young mothers, as well as the conditions of life waiting for children born into poverty or an abusive home. So at the outset of any conversation about abortion, realize that it will be difficult and potentially even explosive.

Each year when I teach the abortion cases to my Constitutional Law classes, I remind the students of this background and admonish them to keep in mind that some of their classmates may have a real and possibly very painful experience with abortion and that their comments on the cases and the debates should be made with that in mind. But I still teach the cases and we still have the debates and discussions, as should every citizen who cares about the country.

Begin with this obvious fact: If *Roe v. Wade* had not been handed down in 1973, there would most assuredly be millions more Americans today than there are. Even with liberalized abortion laws of the sort that were evolving in the early '70s, the complete overthrow of the nation's complicated and generally restrictive abortion laws more than a third of a century ago launched a massive utilization of the procedure that led to easy availability of abortion and thus to a much lower population today than we would otherwise have had.

As noted, we also have millions of women whose lives have been marked by the decision to obtain an abortion. For many of these women, the decision has no emotional significance and has had no long-term impact on their lives. For many others, the opposite is true. I have spoken at enough crisis pregnancy center fundraisers and have heard the testimony of enough women who deeply regret their past choices to know that abortion can fundamentally upend a woman's life even as it completely ends the life in the womb.

There are other consequences as well, including the revolution in sexual mores launched by the combination of easily accessible birth control and the failsafe guarantee of abortion should birth control fail or be forgotten. And of course the country's politics have been deeply distorted by the three-plus decades of arguments and recriminations.

All of these issues and many more complicate and often sidetrack conversations about abortion.

For this week's study though, there is a much more basic question: What does God say about unborn children? Does God approve of abortion? Is He neutral about the practice? Does abortion equal sin, and if so, of what sort? Does complacency about abortion also equal sin? Can a Christian in good conscience choose to avoid the issue because of its many sensitivities? Can a Christian vote for a pro-abortion rights politician on the grounds that other issues trump this one?

In his 2008 book, *Render Unto Caesar*, the Roman Catholic Archbishop of Denver, Charles Chaput, made a strong case for awakening voters to the moral weight of their vote on the issue of abortion. Abortion was not just one issue among many, Chaput argued, but the most important issue of all, far overshadowing other debates. The archbishop also rejected attempts to sidestep the debate by arguing about capitol punishment or just war debates, noting the scale of the abortions in the country. Chaput's arguments were echoed by many other senior Roman Catholic prelates prior to the election, and no leader in the Roman Catholic Church even whispered a contrary view, so clear is Roman Catholic teaching on this subject.

But as we saw at the start of this book, millions of mass-attending, devout Catholics ignored the guidance of their leaders and voted for President Obama, surely the most abortion-rights friendly candidate for president ever. So this is the bottom-line question to discuss today: When you stand before God and Christ for your final judgment, do you imagine part of that judgment will be your action or inaction with regard to abortion? Are you relying on the atoning mission of Christ to cover your record on this issue, or does it not even enter into your consideration of your own sinfulness? And if God is indeed outraged by the loss of millions and millions of lives cut short of their full flower, ought you to be outraged as well, and should you be active somehow in ending the practice? On a very personal level, should you at least support the efforts of a crisis pregnancy center to provide alternatives to abortion? Should you on a personal level at least be trying to save one life or more through an investment of time or money? And should your voting reflect your thoughtful consideration of these questions?

Week 7:
Can Politics Feed the Hungry and Clothe the Naked?

Scripture:

I know that the LORD secures justice for the poor and upholds the cause of the needy.

—Psalm 140:12

Do not withhold good from those who deserve it, when it is in your power to act. Do not say to your neighbor, "come back later; I'll give it tomorrow" when you now have it with you.

—Proverbs 3:27-28

For even when we were with you, we gave you this rule: "If a man will not work, he shall not eat."

—2 Thessalonians 3:10

When the Son of Man comes in His glory, and all the holy angels with Him, then He will sit on the throne of His glory. All the nations will be gathered before Him, and He will separate them one from another, as a shepherd divides his sheep from the goats. And He will set the sheep on His right hand, but the goats on the left. Then the King will say to those on His right hand, "Come, you blessed of My Father, inherit the kingdom prepared for you from the foundation of the world: for I was hungry and you gave Me food; I was thirsty and you gave Me drink; I was a stranger and you took Me in; I was naked and you clothed Me; I was sick and you visited Me; I was in prison and you came to Me."

Then the righteous will answer Him, saying, "Lord, when did we see You hungry and feed You, or thirsty and give You drink? When did we see You a stranger and take You in, or naked and clothe You? Or when did we see You sick, or in prison, and come to You?" And the King will answer and say to them, "Assuredly, I say to you, inasmuch as you did it to one of the least of these My brethren, you did it to Me."

Then He will also say to those on the left hand, "Depart from Me, you cursed, into the everlasting fire prepared for the devil and his angels: for I was hungry and you gave Me no food; I was thirsty and you gave Me no drink; I was a stranger and you did not take Me in, naked and you did not clothe Me, sick and in prison and you did not visit Me."

Then they also will answer Him, saying, "Lord, when did we see You hungry or thirsty or a stranger or naked or sick or in prison, and did not minister to You?"

Then He will answer them, saying, "Assuredly, I say to you, inasmuch as you did not do it to one of the least of these, you did not do it to Me." And these will go away into everlasting punishment, but the righteous into eternal life.

—Matthew 25:31-46

Readings:

At the end of life, we will not be judged by how many diplomas we have received, how much money we have made, how many great things we have done. We will be judged by "I was hungry, and you gave me something to eat, I was naked and you clothed me. I was homeless, and you took me in." Hungry not only for bread—but hungry for love. Naked not only for clothing—but naked of human dignity and respect. Homeless not only for want of a home of bricks—but homeless because of rejection.

—Mother Teresa

We are a humane and generous people and we accept without reservation our obligation to help the aged, disabled, and those unfortunates who, through no fault of their own, must depend on their fellow man. But we are not going to perpetuate poverty by substituting a permanent dole for a paycheck. There is no humanity or charity in destroying self-reliance, dignity, and self-respect—the very substance of moral fiber.

—Ronald Reagan

Although liberal families' incomes average 6 percent higher than those of conservative families, conservative-headed households give, on average, 30 percent more to charity than the average liberal-headed household... While conservatives tend to regard giving as a personal rather than governmental responsibility, some liberals consider private charity a retrograde phenomenon—a poor palliative for an inadequate welfare state, and a distraction from achieving adequacy by force, by increasing taxes. Ralph Nader, running for president in 2000, said: "A society that has more justice is a society that needs less charity." Brooks, however, warns: "If support for a policy that does not exist ... substitutes for private charity, the needy are left worse off than before. It is one of the bitterest ironies of liberal politics today that political opinions are apparently taking the place of help for others."

—George Will

Commentary and Questions:

So, what do you do for the poor, really? Do the taxes you pay have anything at all to do with what Christ commands us about the poor? Does our political orientation tell us anything about our concern for and care of the poor? Or are exclamations about how we need a different tax policy or spending priorities a poor substitute for personal action vis-à-vis the poor?

Many Christians believe they should support candidates who are pledged to more programs directed toward alleviating poverty and easing the burden on the poorest among our society. I have often had callers to my radio show challenge my belief in low tax rates as an indication that my faith is poorly formed. My answer—low taxes lead to robust economic growth, which is the only solution to poverty that works—never satisfies them, probably because they don't believe the premise.

does not work

This is not a discussion guide that is intended to provoke a debate between supply-side, low tax economics, and classic Keynesian dogma. Rather, I'd like to pose the question this way: If we knew which policies promoted the most economic growth, would we be obliged as Christians to support those policies? Or are we obliged as Christians to support those candidates pledged to the most spending on the poor regardless of the consequences to the overall economy?

On these two questions turn many long conversations and millions and millions of votes. Once you are clear on the answers to them, a lot of other debates become easier, though not all. The consequences of government assistance to the poor are not all good, of course, and many scores of good books have looked at the damage done by well-meaning government initiatives that in fact led to greater dependency and such deeply destructive side effects as leaving homes after the government made it profitable to do so.

The debates over specific government initiatives will depend upon the particulars of any initiative and the side effects that initiative will produce. But the overall debate should be shaped by fundamental questions: Is there a Christian approach to economics, and if so, does it value growth for the most or maximum spending on the lost and the least? If there is no clear-cut answer to these questions, should a Christian's political choices turn on other issues on which there are indeed very clear answers?

Doesn't really answer the question

Week 8:
National Security, Part 1:
Is There Such a Thing As A Just War?

Scripture:

Rescue those who are unjustly sentenced to death; don't stand back and let them die. Don't try to avoid responsibility by saying you didn't know about it.
—Proverbs 24:11

This is how we know what love is: Jesus Christ laid down his life for us. And we ought to lay down our lives for our brothers. If anyone has material possessions and sees his brother in need but has no pity on him, how can the love of God be in him? Dear children, let us not love with words or tongue but with actions and in truth.
—1 John 3:16-18

Defend the cause of the weak and fatherless; maintain the rights of the poor and oppressed. Rescue the weak and needy; deliver them from the hand of the wicked.
—Psalm 82:3, 4

Blessed are the peacemakers, for they shall be called the children of God.
—Matthew 5:9

Readings:

War has ended more evil than anything the left has ever thought of. In the last 60 years alone, it ended

Nazism and the Holocaust; it saved half of Korea from genocide; it kept Israel from national extinction and a second Holocaust; it saved Finland from becoming a Stalinist totalitarian state; and according to most of the people who put "War is not the answer" stickers on their bumpers, it saved Bosnian Muslims from ethnic cleansing.

—Dennis Prager

In conclusion, a war, to be just, must be waged by a sovereign power for the security of a perfect *right* of its own (or of another justly invoking its protection) against foreign violation in a case where there is no other means available to secure or repair the *right*; and must be conducted with a moderation which, in the continuance and settlement of the struggle, commits no act intrinsically immoral, nor exceeds in damage done, or in payment and in penalty exacted, the measure of necessity and of proportion to the value of the *right* involved, the cost of the war, and the guarantee of future security.

—Charles Macksey

Again, there are certain duties that we owe even to those who have wronged us. For there is a limit to retribution and to punishment; or rather, I am inclined to think, it is sufficient that the aggressor should be brought to repent of his wrong-doing, in order that he may not repeat the offence and that others may be deterred from doing wrong. Then, too, in the case of a state in its external relations, the rights of war must be strictly observed. For since there are two ways of settling a dispute: first, by discussion; second; by physical force; and since the former is characteristic of man, the latter of the brute, we must resort to force only in case we may not avail ourselves of discussion. The only excuse, therefore, for going to war is that we may live in peace unharmed; and when the victory is won, we should spare those who have not been blood-thirsty and barbarous in their warfare.

—Cicero

None of the four wars in my lifetime came about because we were too strong. It is weakness that invites adventurous adversaries to make mistaken judgments. America is the most peaceful, least warlike nation in modern history. We are not the cause of all the ills of the world. We're a patient and generous people. But for the sake of our freedom and that of others, we cannot permit our reserve to be confused with a lack of resolve.

—Ronald Reagan

The most fundamental paradox is that, if we're never to use force, we must be prepared to use it and to use it successfully. We Americans don't want war, and we don't start fights. We don't maintain a strong military force to conquer or coerce others. The purpose of our military is simple and straightforward: We want to prevent war by deterring others from the aggression that causes war. If our efforts are successful, we will have peace and never be forced into battle. There will never be a need to fire a single shot. That's the paradox of deterrence.

—Ronald Reagan

Not all the treasures of the world, so far as I believe, could have induced me to support an offensive war, for I think it murder; but if a thief breaks into my house, burns and destroys my property, and kills or threatens

to kill me, or those that are in it, and to "bind me in all
cases whatsoever" to his absolute will, am I to suffer it?
—Thomas Paine

Commentary and Questions:

Was the American Civil War a just war? Was World War II?
Vietnam? The 2001 invasion of Afghanistan? The 2003 invasion of Iraq? Are Afghanistan and Iraq better off today than
they were before the American-led invasions and overthrow of
the Taliban and Saddam, respectively?

There is a long and rich debate among theologians over
when, if ever, war can be just. Most mainstream American
Christian leaders agree that there are times when war is indeed
the answer, but every single occasion of America going to war
in the last one hundred-plus years has triggered vigorous opposition from Christian anti-war activists.

What is crucial for the development of a Christian's political identity is a set of first principles which can then be applied
to any particular set of circumstances.

For your discussion today: Should the United States
ever initiate war, and if so, when? Only when the threat is
obvious—al Qaeda operating unmolested in Afghanistan
after 9/11—or more obscure, as with the danger that Saddam
would assist terrorists seeking to strike the United States? How
much should a Christian trust the leaders of a country who will
have access to much more information than ordinary voters
do? When President Bill Clinton ordered the bombing of Iraq
in 1998's Operation Desert Fox—done to degrade Saddam's
alleged WMD programs—or when President Clinton ordered
the massive bombing of Serbia as a means of bringing the
genocidal war against the Kosovars to an end, was he acting
morally? Is there a difference between these two uses of force by
President Clinton and President George Bush's uses of force in
Afghanistan and Iraq? Of course many thousands of Americans

died in the battles after 9/11 and tens of thousands more were severely wounded, but far fewer than were wounded and killed in Vietnam, Korea, or either of the World Wars. Do the casualty counts matter to the larger question of when to use force? How then ought a Christian to assess a candidate's statements about war and the use of military power?

Week 9:
How Much Should the Rich Man Pay?

Scripture:

Jesus looked steadily at him and loved him, and he said, "There is one thing you lack. Go and sell everything you own and give to the poor, and you will have treasure in heaven; then come, follow me." But his face fell at these words and he went away sad, for he was a man of great wealth. Jesus looked around and said to his disciples, "How hard it is for those who have riches to enter the kingdom of God!" The disciples were astounded by these words, but Jesus insisted, "My children," he said to them, "how hard it is to enter the kingdom of God! It is easier for a camel to pass through the eye of a needle than for a rich man to enter the kingdom of God." They were more astonished than ever. "In that case," they said to one another, "who can be saved?" Jesus gazed at them. "For men," he said, "it is impossible, but not for God: because everything is possible for God... Many who are first will be last, and the last first."

—Mark 10:21-27, 31

Rest in the Lord and wait patiently for Him; Do not fret because of him who prospers in his way... Better is the little of the righteous than the abundance of many wicked.

—Psalm 37:7, 16

The Lord sends poverty and wealth; he humbles and he exalts.

—1 Sam 2:7

Readings:

You say the rich will leave the country rather than face a marginal tax of 50 percent? Let them, and take away their citizenship.

—Robert Reich

Property is the fruit of labor... property is desirable... is a positive good in the world. That some should be rich shows that others may become rich, and hence is just encouragement to industry and enterprise. Let not him who is houseless pull down the house of another; but let him labor diligently and build one for himself, thus by example assuring that his own shall be safe from violence when built.

—Abraham Lincoln

That the rich have a duty to alleviate the sufferings of the poor is well attested in Scripture and the Tradition. St. Thomas teaches, following St. Ambrose, that one has a duty to give out of any superfluous wealth to relieve the plight of the poor. But the poor have a duty as well, that of Gratitude. St. Thomas teaches that Gratitude is a virtue, and that one to whom a kindness has been done has an obligation to reciprocate it. He says, following Aristotle, that "we should do a kindness in turn to one who has been kind to us." If the poor who have received a kindness have a duty to turn around and "go do likewise," implied is the idea that they will be in a position to do a favor, which further implies that their circumstances will be remedied to some extent. Therefore the ability to "go and do likewise," necessitates that the poor will be reformed. Now if God wills the end that the poor will be able to render favors, then He must will the means of this coming to be. The means of the reformation of the poor is the Grace of God, given through the mediation of the Body of Christ. The members of the Body minister to each other, and each to the other is an image and sign of Christ's Grace... thus the Church becomes the agency of real transformation.

—Robert Johansen

Though the earth, and all inferior creatures, be common to all men, yet every man has a **property** in his own **person**: this nobody has any right to but himself. The **labour** of his body, and the work of his hands, we may say, are properly his.

—John Locke

In America, I have never met a citizen so poor that he did not cast a glance of hope and envy toward the pleasures of the rich or whose imagination did not anticipate the good things which fate stubbornly refused to him. Alternatively, I have never observed among the wealthy of the United States that arrogant contempt for material prosperity which sometimes manifests itself in the most opulent and dissolute aristocracies. Most of these wealthy men have been poor and felt the sharp sting of necessity. For many years they have battle against a hostile fate and, now that victory is won, the passions which accompanied the struggle stay with them. They remain almost drunk on the trivial delights they have pursued for forty years. Not that in the United States, as elsewhere, you do not encounter quite a large number of wealthy people who have inherited their possessions and enjoy, without the need for effort, wealthy they have not earned. But even these appear to be no less attached to the delights of the material world. The love of comfort has become the dominant taste of the nation. The main current of human passions runs in that channel and sweeping all before it in its course.

—Alexis De Tocqueville

Tax rates are prices—prices for working, saving, and investing. And when you raise the price of those productive activities, you get less of them and more activity in the underground economy, tax shelters, and leisure pursuits. You in small business understand that you can't force people to buy merchandise that isn't selling by raising your price. But too many in Washington and across the country still believe that we can raise more revenue from the economy by making it more expensive to work, save, and invest in the economy. We can't repeal human nature.

—Ronald Reagan

Like federal employees, taxpayers also work for the government—they just don't have to take a civil service exam. Here in America, land of opportunity, governments at all levels are taxing away 40 percent of our nation's income. We've been creeping closer to socialism, a system that someone once said works only in heaven, where it isn't needed, and in hell, where they've already got it.

—Ronald Reagan

Will Rogers once said he never met a man he didn't like. Well, if I could paraphrase Will, our friends in the other party have never met a tax they didn't like or hike.

—Ronald Reagan

Commentary and Questions:

An earlier chapter asked the question of whether there is such a thing as Christian economics. This week's discussion asks a much narrower question that really applies only to very few people: How much of a wealthy man's or woman's money should a Christian support the government taking as a matter not of good economic policy but of justice? Since the preservation of wealth depends upon there being a government that can stop criminals from stealing and enemies from destroying savings and property, should the wealthy as a matter of course be taxed at much higher rates than the merely well-off?

This is a discussion that looks at inheritance taxes and wealth taxes and the idea, voiced by President Obama to the fleetingly famous "Joe the Plumber" of "spreading the wealth around."

As a matter of morals, should the government take a great deal from the very wealthy and put it into other projects simply because it is wrong in a democracy for anyone to control great, great sums of money? Should a Christian, as a matter of the moral health of the taxed and of the whole community, urge the absorption by the government of great estates down to some manageable level? Should the Christian support limits on executive pay and luxury taxes on expensive pastimes like yachts and fourth homes? Or should a Christian leave that to God and the individual to work out?

American capitalism is so deeply ingrained in our habits of thinking that only rarely do we ask ourselves about the morality of allowing great concentrations of wealth to pass from generation to generation, deepening income inequality and perhaps fraying the civic ties that bind us together. Assume for the purpose of discussion that high taxes on big estates would not greatly or at all impact overall economic growth. If that was indeed the case, should Christians support taking a large part of a person's wealth away from them for the benefit of their soul? If not, aren't we denying the clear teaching of Scripture and demonstrating indifference to the soul-destroying conditions of great wealth?

Week 10:
What Does "Stewardship of the Earth" Mean?

Scripture:

God blessed them and said to them, "Be fruitful and increase in number; fill the earth and subdue it. Rule over the fish of the sea and the birds of the air and over every living creature that moves on the ground."

—Genesis 1:26, 28

And he said to him, "Well done, good servant; because you were faithful in a very little, have authority over ten cities."

—Luke 19:17

Readings:

Respect for creation is, for Christians, based in the worship of the Creator. Despoilers of nature are unfaithful stewards of creation. We are to treat all creation—and all creatures—with respect and thankfulness. But, we are not to confuse plants and animals with humans. Humans have rights because human beings are made in the image of God. Plants do not have rights.

—Dr. Albert Mohler

Yes, we should take care of the environment. But most of all, we should take care of our souls. Is Christ the center of your life, and are you seeking to live for Him every day?

—Billy Graham

For he has raised everywhere, in all places and in all things, his ensigns and emblems, under blazons so clear and intelligible that no one can pretend ignorance in not knowing such a sovereign Lord... It is evident that all creatures, from those in the firmament to those which are in the center of the earth, are able to act as witnesses and messengers of his glory to all men.... For the little birds that sing, sing of God; the beasts clamor for him; the elements dread him, the mountains echo him, the mountains and flowing waters cast their glances at him, and the grass and flowers laugh before him.

In grasses, trees, and fruits, apart from their various uses, there is beauty of appearance and pleasantness of odor.... Has the Lord clothed the flowers with the great beauty that greets our eyes, the sweetness of smell that is wafted upon our nostrils, and yet will it be unlawful for our eyes to be affected by that beauty, or our sense of smell by the sweetness of that odor?... Did he not, in short, render many things attractive to us, apart from their necessary use? While it is true that God declares Himself to us by His Word, nevertheless we are inexcusable when we have not at all considered Him in His works... Let us note then that St. Paul says, (Acts 14:17) that when God causes the sun to shine, sends the diverse seasons, fructifies the earth, that He does not at all leave Himself without good testimony... Let us then only open our eyes and we will have enough arguments for the grandeur of God, so that we may learn to honor Him as He deserves.

—John Calvin

If I am going to be in the right relationship with God, I should treat the things he has made in the same way he treats them.

—Francis Schaeffer

The tree in the field is to be treated with respect. It is not to be romanticized, as the old lady romanticizes her cat (that is, she reads human reactions into it). This is wrong because it is not true. When you drive the axe into the tree when you need firewood, you are not cutting down a person; you are cutting down a tree. But while we realize we should not romanticize the **tree**, we must realize that God made it and it deserves respect because He made it a tree. Christians who do not believe in the complete evolutionary scale have reason to respect nature as the total evolutionist never can, because we believe God made these things specifically in their own areas. So if we are going to argue against the evolutionists intellectually, we should show the results of our beliefs in our attitudes. The Christian is a man who has a reason for dealing with each created thing with a high level of respect.

—Francis Schaeffer

We affirm that God-given dominion is a sacred responsibility to steward the earth and not a license to abuse the creation of which we are a part. Because clean air, pure water, and adequate resources are crucial to public health and civic order, government has an obligation to protect its citizens from the effects of environmental degradation.

—The National Association of Evangelicals'
"Evangelical Call to Civic Responsibility"

Commentary and Questions:

In the past decade, concern over global warming has entered the popular consciousness, and many millions of Christian have argued that it is a requirement of faithfulness to the gospel that individual Christians act decisively to slow the emission of carbon into the atmosphere. This trend became most pronounced when many Anglican congregations in Great Britain suggested to their members during Lent in 2008 that they "give up" carbon-emitting activities as a penitential practice.

The rhetoric of environmentalism often ends up as heated as the planet is allegedly becoming, with predictions of doom around the corner. What do you believe about global warming?

One "moderate" view is that the earth has been warming, but we don't know how much and we don't know how much humans contribute to the warming, or what could be done about it in any event. Another "moderate view" is that unnecessary risks in this area should be avoided and all possible reductions achieved because the stakes are so high. Why would anyone be indifferent to any risk, however slight, if the consequences are so catastrophic?

What's a Christian to do? On the one hand, even regulation enthusiasts admit that the control of carbon emissions is a very expensive undertaking, one that will weigh most heavily on less developed countries with exploding populations that need energy to develop the basic means of survival. Does the protection of the environment mean that the billions of the world's people who live in poverty should simply endure for the benefit of the overall race over the long haul?

Or should a Western Christian recognize that we in America consume vastly greater amounts of energy than our counterparts around the world and that we simply have to cutback dramatically? Do advocates of such cutbacks ignore the consequences of less production of food, medicine, and technology on the global population? America uses so much energy because it produces so many goods. Cut back on American productivity and you cut back on the technological progress that feeds and cures the world.

Does anyone have a right to judge the actions of individuals as sinful or acceptable in the absence of an agreed upon plan of action that is embraced and enforced across the planet? Can gestures ever have moral significance? Finally, does the use of more energy than necessary constitute sin? Does God oblige us to keep the thermostat at any particular temperature or to drive any particular car? Or does that discussion divert us from far more real sins of indifference to suffering a few miles from our house? If all of the effort that went into global warming debates instead went into World Vision or Children's International sponsorships of children and responsible development in impoverished foreign lands, wouldn't the globe be better off and our Christian responsibilities of stewardship more carefully and rightfully exercised?

Week 11:
Do You Care About the Courts?

Scripture:

Speak up for those who cannot speak for themselves, for the rights of all who are destitute. Speak up and judge fairly; defend the rights of the poor and needy.

—Proverbs 31:8, 9

Now let the fear of the Lord be upon you. Judge carefully, for with the Lord our God there is no injustice or partiality or bribery.

—2 Chronicles 19:15

Readings:

I don't think that government has a role in telling people how to live their lives. Maybe a minister does, maybe your belief in God does, maybe there's another set of moral codes, but I don't think government has a role.

—Clarence Thomas

It is, therefore, ominous news that the rule of law has become confused with—indeed subverted by—by the rule of judges. That subversion is precisely what judicial activism accomplishes.

—Robert Bork

I believe there are more instances of the abridgement of the freedom of the people by gradual and silent encroachments of those in power than by violent and sudden usurpation.

—James Madison

Now the Senate is looking for moderate judges, mainstream judges. What in the world is a moderate interpretation of a constitutional text? Halfway between what it says and what we'd like it to say?

—Justice Antonin Scalia

If you think the Constitution is some exhortation to give effect to the most fundamental values of the society as those values change from year to year... If you think it is simply meant to reflect the evolving standards of decency that mark the progress of a maturing society— if that is what you think it is, then why in the world would you have it interpreted by nine lawyers? What do I know about the evolving standards of decency of American society? I'm afraid to ask.

—Justice Antonin Scalia

It cannot be overstated, Mike. If we go back and read the writings of the framers of the Constitution, it becomes very clear that they feared the tendency of man to grab power and to subvert the tenets of democracy. And that's why they set up a system of checks and balances: to keep one branch of the federal government from overpowering and dominating the other two. That system has worked very well between the legislative and the executive branches. But the judiciary has not been checked by the Congress in the way that the Constitution prescribed. Therefore the courts are totally out of control. You know, the courts now make every important moral decision, and they interfere with more and more of our private lives. These black-robed judges are unelected and unaccountable and arrogant and we must curtail their power.

—James Dobson

Thanks to liberal decisions made by the Court over the past thirty-odd years, the culture wars have enflamed public opinion and divided Americans. Debates over gay marriage, abortion, and public expressions of religiosity—at best, deeply controversial—were exacerbated and prolonged by the Supreme Court's forays into policymaking. While the legislative process forges consensus by allowing all voices to be heard, judicial fiat leaves no room for compromise. It is impossible to craft law without extended dialogue, and a great deal of give and take. When social policy is left to the Court, it does not matter whether decisions are made in the spirit of compromise; the first casualty of such decisions is polity.

—Nathan Tabor

Rejecting the idea of a "living Constitution" simply means that a Justice will respect the authority allotted to the legislative and executive branches (and the state governments) by the actual language of the Constitution and will not create new "rights" out of thin air. A Supreme Court Justice should fairly and impartially interpret the Constitution in light of the original meaning of its language, not seek to advance a social agenda by legislating from the bench.

—Jay Sekulow

The framers of the constitution contemplated that instrument, as a rule for the government of courts, as well as of the legislature... Why otherwise does it direct the judges to take an oath to support it? This oath certainly applies, in an especial manner, to their conduct in their official character. How immoral to impose it on them, if they were to be used as the instruments, and

the knowing instruments, for violating what they swear
to support! (Marbury v. Madison)
—Chief Justice John Marshall

Commentary and Questions:

Rarely does American politics become focused on who will
be wearing the robes on this or that court. When it does, it
is usually because there is a vacancy on the Supreme Court
and a nominee to fill it—most recently Associate Justice Sonia
Sotomayor—one who undergoes confirmation hearings before
the Judiciary Committee of the United States Senate, hearings
which inevitably involve the topic of abortion since abortion
has been the province of the courts since 1973.

Of course, judges and especially the justices of the United
States Supreme Court decide much more than when and if abortion is available in the United States. They decide how property is controlled, whether guns are available, whether people
suspected of terrorism get trials, whether marijuana is available
to those who want it to ease suffering, whether pornography
can be kept out of public libraries, where churches are located
and how big they can be, and hundreds of thousands of other
cases and controversies as well.

Is there a Christian attitude toward judges? If so, it will
have consequences on how you vote as there is clearly a huge
division between the major parties on this front. Republicans
generally, and their highest-profile nominees almost always,
support an approach to judging known as "originalism," and
are thus committed to a very narrow approach to judging.
These sorts of judges try and refer the big issues back to elected
representatives unless a clear answer on how to decide an issue
is obvious on the face of the Constitution or a statute passed by
Congress and signed by the president. Almost all "originalist"
judges think ***Roe v. Wade*** was wrongly decided, and would

uphold restrictions on abortion passed by state legislatures and the Congress, and many would reverse *Roe* entirely.

Democrats, by contrast, support "activist" judges who believe their jobs should involve pushing forward rules that equalize conditions in America and reverse the effects of past failings such as racial discrimination and discrimination against women. Activist judges are result-oriented and do not shy away from finding reasons to order the changes they think will benefit society. They are less concerned with the rights of private property owners, less worried about the rights of gun owners, and dedicated to the easy availability of abortion and are thus hostile to restrictions on abortion from Congress or state legislatures.

This is a simplification of the very complex explanation of the differences between originalist and activist judges, but it is a fair, short summary, especially on the jurisprudence of abortion, pornography, and property and gun rights.

Given this very clear distinction between the parties, should a Christian be predisposed toward a Republican or Democratic candidate for the presidency or the United States Senate on the basis of their likely approach to judicial nominees and confirmations? If we are called to be serious opponents of abortion or pornography, aren't Christians obliged to take these differences between the parties seriously when voting? Or does an activist judge's solicitude for the rights of the long oppressed oblige us to set aside their activism in other areas that can be influenced through other means and hope for their appointment and domination of the bench?

Week 12:
Do We Need Borders?

Scripture:

Do not move an ancient boundary stone set up by your forefathers.

—Proverbs 22:28

Therefore, it is necessary to submit to the authorities, not only because of possible punishment but also because of conscience. This is also why you pay taxes, for the authorities are God's servants, who give their full time to governing. Give everyone what you owe him: If you owe taxes, pay taxes; if revenue, then revenue; if respect, then respect; if honor, then honor.

—Romans 13:5-7

Do not deprive the alien or the fatherless of justice, or take the cloak of the widow as a pledge. Remember that you were slaves in Egypt and the LORD your God redeemed you from there. That is why I command you to do this. When you are harvesting in your field and you overlook a sheaf, do not go back to get it. Leave it for the alien, the fatherless and the widow, so that the LORD your God may bless you in all the work of your hands. When you beat the olives from your trees, do not go over the branches a second time. Leave what remains for the alien, the fatherless and the widow. When you harvest the grapes in your vineyard, do not go over the vines again. Leave what remains for the alien, the fatherless and the widow. Remember that you were slaves in Egypt. That is why I command you to do this.

—Deuteronomy 24:17-22

Readings:

During the heyday of multiculturalism and political correctness in the 1980s, the response of us, the hosts, to this novel challenge was not to insist upon the traditional assimilation of the newcomer but rather to accommodate the illegal alien with official Spanish-language documents, bilingual education, and ethnic boosterism in our media, politics, and education. These responses only encouraged more illegals to come, on the guarantee that their material life could be better and yet their culture unchanged in the United States. We now see the results. Los Angeles is today the second largest Mexican city in the world; one out of every ten Mexican nationals resides in the United States, the vast majority illegally.

—Victor Davis Hanson

Against the insidious wiles of foreign influence, (I conjure you to believe me fellow citizens) the jealousy of a free people ought to be constantly awake; since history and experience prove that foreign influence is one of the most baneful foes of Republican Government.

—George Washington

Commentary and Questions:

This week and next, the study concerns America's borders. Before you leap to the conclusion that of course we need borders, ask yourself if Christ agrees. Almost all Americans will at least agree in theory to borders as a necessity in the age of terror and drug trafficking, but what does Christ say about the subject? Should a Christian support the idea that international order requires the rich keep out the poor? Or should we be at least committed in theory to the free travel of all everywhere they want to go in search of a better life?

Note that the rich can almost always go anywhere in the world they want to reach, but the poor have difficulty crossing even local borders. Is this the world we are called to create? If borders are a necessity of international stability and safety, are Christians in the developed world at least called to double and triple their efforts to bring the advantages of development to the impoverished parts of the globe and to do so personally? Does a Christian voter need to consider the international aid platforms of candidates, and to know the facts of an incumbent's record on such matters as the provision of AIDS drugs to Africa and food aid to North Korea?

Week 13:
What About Illegal Immigrants?

Scripture:

The same law applies to the native-born and to the alien living among you.

—Exodus 12:49

Men do not despise a thief if he steals to satisfy his hunger when he is starving. Yet if he is caught, he must pay sevenfold, though it costs him all the wealth of his house.

—Proverbs 6:30-31

Readings:

The influx of foreigners must, therefore, tend to produce a heterogeneous compound; to change and corrupt the national spirit; to complicate and confound public opinion; to introduce foreign propensities. In the composition of society, the harmony of the ingredients is all-important, and whatever tends to a discordant intermixture must have an injurious tendency.

—Alexander Hamilton

...The policy or advantage of [immigration] taking place in a body (I mean the settling of them in a body) may be much questioned; for, by so doing, they retain the language, habits, and principles (good or bad) which they bring with them. Whereas by an intermixture with our people, they, or their descendants, get assimilated to our customs, measures, and laws: in a word, soon become one people.

—George Washington

Citizens by birth or choice of a common country, that country has a right to concentrate your affections. The name of American, which belongs to you, in your national capacity, must always exalt the just pride of Patriotism, more than any appellation derived from local discriminations.

—George Washington

The May Day exercise was greatly revealing. In the first round, most of the hand-held flags were Mexican. Quick sophistication turned many flags into Stars and Stripes for the second round. But the chants were mostly in Spanish, and what they demanded was of course amnesty and citizenship. The eleven million illegals will continue to swell in number, and widespread assimilation won't begin, until the border effectively closes. An argument can be made that this can't happen, that the porosity of the two thousand mile stretch is now almost geologically ordained. Or is this now the accepted challenge? The moon-landing ambition for 2006: closing the border?

—William F. Buckley, Jr.

We find ourselves under the government of a system of political institutions, conducing more essentially to the ends of civil and religious liberty, than any of which the history of former times tells us. We, when mounting the stage of existence, found ourselves the legal inheritors of these fundamental blessings. We toiled not in the acquirement or establishment of them—they are a legacy bequeathed us, by a **once** hardy, brave, and patriotic, but **now** lamented and departed race of ancestors. Their's was the task (and nobly they performed it) to possess themselves, and through themselves, us, of this goodly land; and to uprear upon its hills and its

✳ Contributors

Former *Latter*

valleys, a political edifice of liberty and equal rights; 'tis ours only, to transmit these, the former, unprofaned by the foot of an invader; the latter, undecayed by the lapse of time and untorn by usurpation, to the latest generation that fate shall permit the world to know. This task, gratitude to our fathers, justice to ourselves, duty to posterity, and love for our species in general, all imperatively require us faithfully to perform."

—Abraham Lincoln

Commentary and Questions:

My friend, Archbishop Charles Chaput of Denver, is much loved by conservatives for his forceful and high-profile leadership on behalf of the unborn. I like to remind them that the archbishop is also a forceful and high-profile leader of efforts to assist the millions of people in the United States who entered the country illegally. He is adamant that families not be split up via deportation and that we need to get people "out of the shadows" where the unscrupulous prey upon them and their fears of deportation if discovered.

People who entered the United States broke the law, but did they sin? Do people who want to enforce the law without much mercy by adopting policies of forced repatriation of all who entered illegally themselves violate many of Christ's commands about the poor and the homeless? Is there a Christian view on illegal immigration, and where in the hierarchy of political issues does it come into play? Given the tens of millions of people such policies would affect, doesn't it rank very, very high in the order of issues a Christian must consider when evaluating candidates for office?

Week 14:
Should Christians Care About the Government's Lack of Control on Pornography?

Scripture:

You have heard that it was said, "You shall not commit adultery"; but I say to you, that everyone who looks on a woman to lust for her has committed adultery with her already in his heart.

—Matt. 5:27-28

Readings:

Beyond the legal confusion, some credit the failure of the porn crackdown to the quiet spread of a kind of laissez-faire attitude toward pornography below the level of judges and prosecutors. It may well be that both the Supreme Court and its critics have lagged behind the country. The national mood could be pointing to an uncensored future, envisioned by Justice Brennan, in which consenting adults will be free to decide for themselves what they will read and see.

—*Time Magazine*

Child pornography harms and debases the most defenseless of our citizens. Both the State and Federal Governments have sought to suppress it for many years, only to find it proliferating through the new medium of the Internet. This Court held unconstitutional Congress's previous attempt to meet this new threat, and Congress responded with a carefully crafted attempt to eliminate the First Amendment problems we identified. As far as the provision at issue in this case is concerned, that effort was successful.

—Justice Antonin Scalia

If your child surfs the Web, chances are he or she already has seen pornography—maybe even hard-core porn. More than a decade after the American public started cruising the Web, it is clear that children can find everything from nudity to sites featuring sexual violence and other extremes. For parents, this creates challenges that never existed before: how to keep porn away from young eyes, and what to do when safety measures fail.

—*USA Today*

Commentary and Questions:

No Christian could, in good conscience, support a candidate who supports the production of child pornography, right? If that is the case, and some candidates support judicial nominees whose rulings make it much more difficult to capture and punish the purveyors of child pornography, doesn't that make such a candidate off limit to Christians? More generally, many candidates think porn is not much of an issue for the federal government and they resist efforts to regulate the Internet so as to limit the tidal wave of pornography. Does such indifference matter to a Christian?

Your view on this will almost certainly be impacted by your view of the severity of the sin of lust as practiced via the use of porn. Certainly we are awash in a sea of porn, and anyone with e-mail knows how ubiquitous porn has become and how completely degraded it routinely is. This is not your father's Playboy culture we are dealing with, but a massive volcano of porn of all sorts and shades, all readily available—for free—over the internet. Porn firms are among the Web's most technologically advanced entrepreneurs and the rise of huge free porn sites has dented the old dirty bookstore/raincoat-clad customer paradigm. Porn is widely regarded as an addiction that strikes millions of people, by far mostly men, and which coarsens and dehumanizes its participants. And the fight against it in legislatures has been all but abandoned.

Should a Christian care? Should Christians demand from politicians a commitment to clean up the Internet and reset the boundaries of what is "protected speech" under the United States Constitution? If so, they won't be voting for Democrats given that it is liberal activist judges who have done so much damage to the efforts to control pornography in the past. There is no debate over this. Though the Republican Party has talked a much better game against porn than it has walked while in control of Congress, judges put forward by Republican presidents and supported by Republican senators are far more likely to uphold restrictions on pornography than those nominated by and supported by Democrats.

Should that matter to a voter? And if so, have you ever engaged in any sort of activism when it comes to curtailing the easy availability of porn, other than in efforts to keep it away from your own children via controls on Internet access in your own home? And if you are concerned with the access of your own children to it, why haven't you done anything about the access of other children and adults to the material?

Week 15:
Should the Government Punish Hateful Speech?

Scripture:

But I tell you who hear me: Love your enemies, do good to those who hate you.

—Luke 6:27

The acts of the sinful nature are obvious: sexual immorality, impurity and debauchery; idolatry and witchcraft; hatred, discord, jealousy, fits of rage, selfish ambition, dissensions, factions and envy; drunkenness, orgies, and the like. I warn you, as I did before, that those who live like this will not inherit the kingdom of God.

—Galatians 5:19-21

Readings:

Congress shall make no law respecting an establishment of religion, or prohibiting the free exercise thereof; or abridging the freedom of speech, or of the press; or the right of the people peaceably to assemble, and to petition the government for a redress of grievances.
—First Amendment to the U.S. Constitution

Does anybody seriously believe that "hate speech" prohibitions will be applied to Muslims demonizing Jews, to blacks demonizing whites, or to women demonizing men?

—Thomas Sowell

The whole idea of hate speech has a dubious basis in the law. Hate crime laws set certain groups apart as deserving of special protections. Christians do not defend physical violence against anyone—homosexuals included—and call for the full prosecution of any who would resort to violence or assault. But to label certain forms of assault hate crimes assumes that the motivation to harm one person is more criminal than the motivation to harm another.

When hate crimes are extended to speech, the government sets itself up as a judge of what language or speech is legal or illegal. The logic of the legislation is clear—no criticism of homosexuality is allowable, whatever its form or basis. This would cover not only epithets thrown at homosexuals, but sermons in Christian pulpits against homosexual behavior.

—R. Albert Mohler, Jr.

If liberty means anything at all, it means the right to tell people what they do not want to hear.

—George Orwell

Mankind can hardly be too often reminded, that there was once a man named Socrates, between whom and the legal authorities and public opinion of his time, there took place a memorable collision... This acknowledged master of all the eminent thinkers who have since lived—whose fame, still growing after more than two thousand years, all but outweighs the whole remainder of the names which make his native city illustrious—was put to death by his countrymen, after a judicial conviction, for impiety and immorality... Of these charges the tribunal, there is every ground for believing, honestly found him guilty, and condemned the man who probably of all then born had deserved best of mankind, to be put to death as a criminal.

—John Stuart Mill

Commentary and Questions:

Mark Steyn is an author and columnist, and the favorite guest of the majority of my radio audience. Steyn appears almost every Thursday to start the show. So captivating is his command of the issues and so great his good humor that I replay the interview to open the third hour of the program, a very unusual routine for a talk show, but one made possible by the fact that most listeners will gladly listen to a replay of Steyn; he is that compelling a voice and that quick a wit. If you have not read deeply in Steyn, sample some of his material at www.SteynOnline.com.

Mark is particularly concerned with birthrates and the rising radical Islamization of Europe. He wrote about that in the context of a book review of author Robert Ferrigno's sci-fi thriller set in the not-so-distant future when American has been split by civil war and nuclear attacks, and the largest bit of the country has converted to Islam. In his trilogy of novels, Ferrigno painted a bleak picture of life under Islamist rule, a picture that Steyn elaborated on in a review carried in the Canadian weekly news magazine *Maclean's* in its February 23, 2006, issue.

The Canadian Islamic Congress objected to what Steyn had written (and many other articles published by *Maclean's*), deeming it "hate speech," and filed a complaint with a Canadian "human rights" tribunal. This launched a long, wearying, and expensive judicial proceeding which, though it exonerated Steyn, did much to burden his life and lighten his purse. It is impossible to say how great the impact of this show trial was on other less well-known figures not as capable as Steyn of mounting a vigorous defense of their right to speak freely about

Radical Islam, but it is fair to suspect that Steyn's ordeal erased quite a few columns and essays not yet published. Who needs that kind of grief?

Christians, of course, are called to be evangelical. Jesus gave His disciples a "Great Commission" and directed them to bring the world the Good News of His saving mission. "Mere Christianity" is also quite clear about how one obtains salvation—through the person of Jesus Christ. The details of this process differ greatly in the minds of the vast number of Christian denominations, but even the centuries-old divide between Protestants and Catholics is nothing compared with the vast gulf between Christians and all other faiths that deny the divinity of Jesus. "Fully God and fully man" is not something that any other religion can agree with, and thus Christians cannot agree with any other religion. They are all in serious error about the nature of the world and of the loving God who calls all men to Himself.

This simple statement of the fact of fundamental disagreement between Christianity and other religions should not be the occasion of anything other than acknowledgment. It is not an authorization for Christians to pursue "forced conversions" which are not conversions at all. It is not an invitation to violence or even hurtful talk.

But there is no escaping a Christian's obligation to be candid in what he or she believes and to tell everyone who asks and many who don't. In the United States, this expression is protected by two parts of the First Amendment to the Constitution—its guarantee to free exercise of religion and its guarantee of free speech. But as Steyn's persecution showed, this is not an international standard, or even a North American one.

And it is by no means secure even here in America. Time and again those intolerant of outspoken Christian speech take steps to silence Christians in the public square.

Sometimes, as when President Obama invited Pastor Rick Warren to offer a prayer at his inauguration in January 2009, voices are raised against the Christian spokesman. In that instance, same-sex marriage proponents unleashed a furious assault on the idea of Warren speaking at the hugely important event. They failed to push Warren from the program, but the marker they put down was unmistakable: Future high-profile events will be blasted by the same special interest group and widely covered by a media very friendly to its agenda. "Hateful speech" like Rick Warren's in defense of traditional marriage will come at a cost.

Other assaults on free speech in the U.S. have been much more direct, in the form of "speech codes" at universities and some "progressive" communities. Expressions of religious conviction or even religious heritage—such as the tiny cross on the seal of Los Angeles County—trigger lawsuits or threats of litigation, and religious speech is censored and the religious symbol often exiled under tortured readings of the First Amendment's ban on the establishment of religion.

The pressure to silence Christianity is increasing, and the militancy of Christianity's opponents—on the one side the harsh voices of the secular left, on the other the radical voices of Islamist fanatics around the globe—push elites toward the easiest path: Pushing the Christians from the public square. Do you care? Do you sigh and turn the page of the newspaper or click the channel when the latest outrage against the traditional symbols of the American indebtedness to Christian beliefs is excised?

If you are alarmed not just by what has happened but also by what seems to be the direction and momentum of future change, you have to know that most of the push against Christian speech comes from the left and is empowered by the courts, and that the center-right that fights back is rooted in the Republican Party and the judicial appointees it champions. If the religion clauses are saved from tortured readings and astonishing applications, it will be because of the coalition of Chief Justice Roberts and Justices Alito, Kennedy, Scalia, and Thomas. As we have seen in earlier weeks' studies and conversations, the future direction of the Supreme Court will be adverse to Christianity if more judicial liberals hostile to religious speech take up posts on the courts. If the elections of 2010, 2012, and beyond don't return balance to the Senate's numbers,

President Obama will rely upon his party's lopsided majority in the Senate to remake the courts into an engine of anti-Christian speech and symbolic expression, and perhaps sooner rather than later find a way to twist some portion of the Constitution into a warrant for "speech codes" that punish statements of moral conviction based upon biblical teaching. Scoff if you wish, but ten years ago, who could have imagined the highest courts in Massachusetts, California, and Connecticut "discovering" mandates for same-sex marriage within the paragraphs of their state constitutions?

Do you think the threat is real? If so, do you care, or ought Christians merely accept that the Great Commission didn't come with a guarantee of ease in the process of speaking? If you do care, what practical steps can be taken to preserve and extend the right to preach the gospel and assure that those who do are not discriminated against?

Week 16:
Should Same-Sex Marriage Be Allowed?

Scripture:

So God created man in His own image; in the image of God He created him; male and female He created them.

—Genesis 1:27

In the same way the men also abandoned natural relations with women and were inflamed with lust for one another. Men committed indecent acts with other men, and received in themselves the due penalty for their perversion.

—Romans 1:27

For this reason a man shall leave his father and mother and be joined to his wife, and the two shall become one flesh.

—Ephesians 5:31

Readings:

Marriage is not created by government. It is older than the Constitution, older than America, older even than the church. It exists in every known human society and it always has something to do with bringing men and women together so that society has the next generation it needs and children have both mothers and fathers, as they need... Two men might each be a good father, but neither can be a mom. Children are hungry for the love and attention of both their parents—their mom and their dad. Marriage is about giving children the ideal, and no same-sex couple can provide that.

—Maggie Gallagher

There is no fact that has been established by social science literature more convincingly than the following: all variables considered, children are best served when reared in a home with a married mother and father.

—A. Dean Byrd, Ph.D.

Wherein one cannot but admire the wisdom of the great Creator, who having given to man foresight, and an ability to lay up for the future, as well as to supply the present necessity, hath made it necessary, that **society of man and wife should be more lasting**, than of male and female of amongst other creatures; that so their industry might be encouraged, and their interest better united, to make provision and lay up goods for their common issue, which uncertain mixture, or easy and frequent solutions of conjugal society would mightily disturb. For all the ends of **marriage** being to be obtained under political government, as well as in the state of nature, the civil magistrate doth not abridge the right or power of either naturally necessary to those ends, viz. procreation and mutual support and assistance whilst they are together; but only decides any controversy that may arise between man and wife about them.

—John Locke

Commentary and Questions:

Other than the presidential election, no issue received more attention from the political press in 2008 than that of same-sex marriage. In May of that year, the California Supreme Court declared that the California state constitution, with previously undiscovered clarity, mandated that "sexual orientation" was a "suspect class" just as race and religion are, and that as such, the denial of marriage to two people of the same sex created an unconstitutional denial of equal protection of the law. The California Supreme Court directed that marriages between two men or two women begin immediately.

Less than six months later, the voters of California delivered a stern rebuke to the would-be judicial emperors. (The case had been decided by a four to three vote.) By more than 52%, the voters amended the Constitution to explicitly state that marriage in the Golden State was between one man and one woman. The victory was achieved despite a bare-knuckled intervention by California Attorney General Jerry Brown that rewrote the amendment's title to make it less appealing and more confusing, and a mainstream media that launched massive free media campaigns against Proposition 8.

The aftermath of the amendment's victory and the return of traditional marriage was as ugly as any domestic political battle of the last forty years—since the violence against civil rights marchers of the 1960s or the bombing attacks of the Weather Underground during Vietnam. Mormons were particular targets of the hate, and terrorist attacks occurred at two Mormon temples though the white powder sent there by same-sex marriage proponents wasn't deadly. A new McCarthyism erupted, but this from the left, as proponents of traditional marriage were driven from their jobs and their businesses were targeted. Contributors to the "Yes on 8" campaign faced relentless verbal and written campaigns of abuse and vilification which blistered into an assault on Pastor Rick Warren, one of mainstream Christianity's most popular and widely admired evangelical voices and a powerful engine for kindness and grace in the world.

The great snarl that erupted in the aftermath of Proposition 8's victory shocked many in the center of the political spectrum and even on the center-right: When did support for marriage based upon religious convictions become so controversial?

When did the tactics of the brownshirts show up in the cause of gay rights?

The puzzlement of many was simply the result of not paying attention over the years as the push for radical secularization of the culture accelerated. Support for gay rights—a widely accepted point of view in the aftermath of the AIDs epidemic—had always been understood as the demand for an absence of hurtful discrimination, and was believed by most people regardless of political ideology to be able to coexist with reasonable accommodations to ordinary conventions such as the "don't ask, don't tell" law for the military and the prohibition of gay scoutmasters within the Boy Scouts. These seem imminently reasonable to many pro-gay rights people as compromises between competing values and long experience of responsible people.

But they were not compromises acceptable to those gay rights advocates who routinely denounced proponents of anything other than their full agenda as "homophobes," and who refused to recognize that society has a strong interest in regulating sexual conduct in many settings. For the same reason that heterosexual young men do not serve as scoutmasters for teenage girl scouts, same-sex attracted young men should not serve as scoutmasters for teenage boys. The long experience of military commanders dictated that unit cohesion not include same-sex attracted men in close quarters with those who were not. Neither of these propositions struck huge numbers of people as homophobic, including millions of people who know and love gay and lesbian people and support for them the right to have visitation of partners guaranteed in times of illness, rights to fair consideration for employment, etc.

The left has no intention of accepting this series of compromises, as the debate and aftermath of Prop. 8 demonstrated. Christians, then, have to decide whether the clear teaching of Scripture—that sexual intimacy is reserved for men and women within the bounds of marriage and outside of those bounds constitute sin of the most serious, soul-destroying, and damnation-inviting kind—matter anymore. Can they simply choose to ignore what they are commanded to believe, and can they stop urging their friends and loved ones to "go and sin no more," even as they work to strengthen their own and others' marriages?

How about you? Do you care? If you live in California, did you vote for or against Proposition 8? Did you make your point of view known, and if not, why not? If you don't live in California, do you live in one of the nearly three dozen states that have seen such a debate in recent years, and if so, what part did you play? Can Christians be silent on this? And does the position of elected officials on this issue matter in your decision on whether to vote for them or not? Though President Obama has stated that he is against same-sex marriage, he also openly campaigned against Proposition 8, an example of having it both ways if there ever was one in politics. The judges he appoints will be overwhelmingly sympathetic to the interpretations that fuel judicial overreaches like that in California. So voting for Obama in 2012 is clearly a vote against traditional marriage. How important is marriage, anyway? And if it is the key building block of western civilization and the guarantor of the family and thus of the country, can a Christian be other than committed to using all legal means to preserve the central institution of the society?

Week 17:
Life Issues, Part 2:
What About Stem Cell Research?

Scripture:

For You formed my inward parts; You covered me in my mother's womb. I will praise You, for I am fearfully and wonderfully made; Marvelous are Your works, And that my soul knows very well.

My frame was not hidden from You, When I was made in secret, And skillfully wrought in the lowest parts of the earth. Your eyes saw my substance, being yet unformed. And in Your book they all were written. The days fashioned for me, When as yet there were none of them.

—Psalm 139:13-16

Reading:

In the process of harvesting embryonic stem cells, the embryo is destroyed. The primary ethical question raised is whether embryos are people or property.

—From the Heritage Foundation

Those human beings who permanently lack certain empowering cognitive capacities—as well as all human beings in stages of life where those powers are absent—are simply the weakest and most needy members of our community. We can care for them and about them only by acknowledging the living bodily presence that they have among us—seeking to discern in their faces the hidden spirit, the call to community that their bodily presence constitutes, and the face of Christ.

—Gilbert Meilaender

The difference between the adult and the child, or the child and the embryo, is merely the gradual development of the same basic natural capacity. But the difference between how we should treat a person (i.e., a being who has intrinsic value and a right to life) and how we may treat an entity that is not a person, and may therefore legitimately be used and even destroyed for the benefit of persons, is a difference that can be morally justified only in virtue of a difference in kind between the person and the nonpersonal entity. Mere differences of degree cannot bear the moral weight required to justify treating some beings possessing the capacity (e.g., normal adults or adolescents) as having dignity and rights while treating other beings possessing the capacity in a lesser, or less developed, degree (e.g., human beings in the embryonic, fetal, or infant stages, mentally retarded people, victims of dementia or Alzheimer's disease) as lacking dignity and a right to life.

—Professor Robert P. George

When Hollywood celebrities describe how their diseases and injuries may benefit from the sacrifice of embryonic life, we are touched by their personal circumstances. But there is another compelling story that must also be told. It is what we would hear if the tiny babies we are about to kill could by some miracle be transformed into a mature adult state, and then begin to plead for their lives. Tens of thousands of voices would blend into a chorus, each saying, "Please let us have our chance. We are human beings, too!" That "other story" would be just as compelling, or more so, as the deeply moving appeals of Mr. Reeve, Ms. Moore and Mr. Fox. It is up to us in the pro-life community to give voice to the voiceless.

—Dr. James Dobson

To take up the questions of medical ethics for probing, to try to enter into the heart of these problems with reasonable and compassionate moral reflection, is to engage in the greatest of joint ventures: the moral becoming of man. This is to see in the prism of medical cases the claims of any man to be honored and respected. So might we enter thoughtfully and actively into the moral history of mankind's fidelity to covenants. In this everyone is engaged.

—Paul Ramsey

First, we are morally capable creatures, accountable beings. We should assume responsibility for what we are doing, and we go wrong when we seek to deny our agency. Not every outcome in stem cell research is foregone; we may shape as well as be shaped by developments, and much may depend on initiatives we take that accord with our own convictions. Second, we are creatures who can exalt ourselves inordinately, i.e., in ways that flout God and manipulate others. This condition is called sin and moral evil in many religious communities… To be tempted to usurp and to do injustice is endemic to human life as we know it. In my own identity as an Augustinian Christian, I take it that we are continually in danger, and that everything is corruptible. If this is right, we should expect that stem cell research is itself not immune to pressures that may usurp and do injustice. In short, we are contending in the case of stem cell research with novel opportunities and challenges, and with permanent capabilities and dangers, and we should try to hold them together as we deliberate.

—Professor Gene Outka

Commentary and Questions

What follows is an interview I conducted with Dr. Frank Turek in late 2008 on the announcement from Speaker Nancy Pelosi that funding embryonic stem cell research would be an early priority in the 2009 Congress.

HH: This past summer I was privileged to go to the Summit Ministries in Colorado Springs and met there a remarkable Christian, intellectual, and apologist, Dr. Frank Turek. He is senior partner of Austin Group in North Carolina. He has been consulting on leadership and management for many years, but he's also quite a thoroughgoing student of the culture. He's got a couple of books out there, *I Don't Have Enough Faith to be an Atheist and Legislating Morality: Is It Wise? Is It Legal? Is It Possible?* I subsequently also learned that Frank is also a naval aviator, which did lead in down in my estimate because Cook is a naval aviator and Damon—guys I know that are naval aviators and they're not much bookish. So, Frank, what did you fly when you were in the Navy?

FT: I was actually on a P3, Hugh. A big, ugly turbo prop that goes out and hunts submarines.

HH: Okay, that's still makes you a naval aviator. I didn't know a whole lot of believers in the Navy when they were flying either. Where you a Christian at the time?

FT: Well, yeah. There's only two kinds. The hard believers and the hard unbelievers, as you know.

HH: Frank, the reason that I got together with you is that I read a story in the *Washington Post* yesterday where Nancy Pelosi announced that on her first week with the new majorities in the House and the Senate, she intends to run through embryonic stem cell research and funding for it. There was a lot of misinformation out there about that and I immediately thought of your book, *Legislating Morality: Is It Wise? Is It Legal?* Is It Possible? and this is one of those issues where morality has been quasi-legislative by George W. Bush. Run us through the significance of this issue and what is at stake from the perspective of a believer.

FT: Well, first of all let me just point out that all laws legislate morality. Every law says one behavior is right and the opposite behavior is wrong, and so laws always put some sort of moral perspective into legal form; whether you're for embryonic stem cell research or not, you're taking a moral point of view and, Hugh, I've got a really bad echo on this line. I don't know if you can hear that or not.

HH: No, you sound great to us.

FT: Anyway, the reason that there is a lot of confusion on this is because—I don't know if your listeners have realized but recently about a year ago there's been a new discovery that takes the whole embryonic stem cell research debate out really of politics—at least it should anyway because they are now able to create the same types of cells from human skin so you don't even need to kill embryos to get the same result. In fact, in last year's

State of the Union Address, President Bush said that he wanted to increase federal funding for embryonic stem cell research that was created by the skin cells and, of course, Republicans leapt to their feet in applause and the Democrats sat on their hands. Now why did they sit on their hands? Because this kind of embryonic stem cell research is something that they didn't want to support. They want to support the kind that, first of all, hasn't given us any advantages. Only adult stem research has given us any advantages. There's been seventy-three treatments from adult stem cell research, Hugh. Zero from embryonic stem cell research.

HH: Let's pause on that for a moment. Seventy-three actual applications of the science gleaned from adult stem cells, zero from embryonic. Is that correct?

FT: Zero from embryonic, the ones we have to kill in embryo. Now as I just mentioned, this new technology is out there and the problem is that politically there's a lot of people who want to affirm the old technology. Why? Because if they affirm it, then they don't admit that an unborn embryo or an embryo itself, a human's zygote, is a human being, see? Because now we're getting into the abortion debate, so there's a political aspect to this that some on that side of the aisle don't want to admit.

HH: Let's stay on that for a moment because I think it is the core issue. People support embryonic stem cell research for two reasons. Some believe it has great potential to heal and others believe that it has potential to end the abortion debate on the side of unlimited opportunity for abortion. Is that a fair statement?

FT: Yeah. I think that some people are worried that if we say there is a moral problem by killing an embryo to get its stem cells, then we are in effect admitting that an unborn child is a human being and that might lead to the end of abortion. Well, we already know that it's a human being. There's no debate scientifically that an unborn child is a human being. That's not the question.

HH: Frank Turek, here goes the question: "But come on, Frank, it's a clump of cells. It has no organs, it can't feel anything. I can understand anti-abortion activists when we're talking about partial-birth abortion or even nearby viability abortion or maybe I'll give you two months, but this is two days, this is one day after conception. This is frozen embryo that might never even be brought to life. Why bother to object?"

FT: Because if we take the functional view of life rather than the essence view of life, where does that end? I mean obviously an unborn child, let's just say a born child, is not really conscious, self-conscious of his or her surroundings. What if we took consciousness or self-awareness as functionality as, say, Dr. Peter Singer from Princeton does. He says that we ought to be able to kill unborn children up to twenty-eight days after they are born—born children, I should say—up to twenty-eight days after they are born. What? Because he takes a functional view rather than a essence view.

HH: What is an "essence" view?

FT: Well, I'm just using that term to say that fundamentally when you have a fertilized ovum, you have a 100% genetic human being. So it's human nature is at that point, as soon as you have a fertilized ovum, you have a human nature—a human essence there.

HH: Now we have seen Nancy Pelosi on *Meet the Press* and Joe Biden on *Meet the Press*; both argue that theology for a long time before the Reformation argued that abortion really wasn't the same moral quandary if it was early enough abortions and, of course, they would argue by extension that even though you have this very small zygote, that you have this very tiny clump of cells, that that's even further removed from the essence of being human. There's no guarantee that it will become human.

FT: Well there's no guarantee that a—well it already is human, that's the point. It's already human, scientifically, from the moment of conception. There's no guarantee that a two-year-old is going to grow up to adulthood either, but we still protect the two-year-old. You are on a slippery slope here if you don't say that something that is genetically a human should have its rights protected. Where do you end? Where do you stop that?

HH: Virginia Postrel, a non-believer I believe—I'm not sure about that, but she's a great libertarian columnist—once argued to me it is the capacity to feel pain that ought to issue forward in a dividing line between acceptable experimentation and non-acceptable experimentation. Your response, Dr. Frank Turek?

FT: A lot of drunk people don't feel pain. Should you be able to experiment on them?

HH: Okay, good point.

FT: What does that prove? I mean unconscious people can't feel pain either; should you be able to cut them open while they are unconscious?

HH: So why is this debate treated like by the media as though it's over, because I don't think it's over. I just think that it has been poorly argued, Frank Turek.

FT: It has been poorly argued because you only get sound bytes in the media and most people on the media are on the left side of the issue, as you know. The interesting thing, Hugh, is, check this out: They criticize Bush for funding stem cell research or for restricting it when he's the only president who's ever put federal dollars behind it. He simply said, "We're going to keep it on these already existing lines that have already been created," and then when this new technology was discovered a year ago, he said, "Let's go there. Let's put more federal money there," and the Democrats were silent about it.

HH: So how do you see this debate? Do you think there are even any people out there that are going to be willing to engage in this or is this going to pass without Republican opposition because they don't want to be thought to be anti-scientific?

FT: Well, actually the Republican opposition they can't do anything because it is an executive order. Obama is just going to get in there and sign it. Now, of course, the Republicans can create a stink and the Republicans can go to the media and Republicans can use their bully pulpit if they have one.

HH: Actually, Nancy Pelosi said she's going to pump up funding on the first day. Yes, the executive order is going to reverse Bush's restrictions—how would you advise them to approach—how would you advise them to set it up, Frank Turek?

FT: Set what up?

HH: The debate. If you're a Republican, you're pro-life, you want to make this argument, how would you advise them to go about it?

FT: Well, I would say first of all I would continue to focus on the humanity of what we're talking about. Are we going to—I don't want to use too extreme an example—but in Nazi Germany, where they were experimenting on humans in order to "benefit humans," that's exactly what we're doing here with embryonic stem cell research. We create a human in order to either harvest its organs or to get stem cells from it and destroying the human in the process. Do we want to go down that road here? And, if this is such a promising line of research, Hugh, why isn't there private funding going into it? Because there's zero benefit that we've seen so far from embryonic stem cell research, plenty of benefit from adult stem cells. Why don't we go there and nobody gets hurt.

HH: Last question, Frank. If someone said, "Zero benefit? I've got to challenge you on that," what would they point us to? You were very good in always knowing the strongest argument on the other side. That impresses me. That's always good for good debaters. What is the best that they can come up with in terms of research into embryonic stem cells?

FT: What embryonic stem cells do, the reason that they are very promising is because at the embryonic level they can become any type of cell we want them to, such as a kidney cell or a heart cell or a lung cell or whatever, so that's where the promise comes in. But the beauty of the new technology is we can create those cells by just taking skin samples from the same person that we want to benefit, and that means that there are no rejection issues either. So, there's just so many benefits for using this new technology I don't see why anyone would want to go back to the old way of doing it, especially when you have these moral problems. The reason they want to go back there, Hugh, is because they know it would be an admission that we need to protect something that's human, and they don't want to go there.

HH: Frank Turek of FrankTurek.com. Thank you, Frank.

—Interview with Dr. Frank Turek
December 4, 2008

Does Dr. Turek persuade you?

Week 18:
Life Issues, Part 3:
Do We Care About Euthanasia?

Scripture:

[handwritten annotation: — PCUSA Mission In Life and Death we Belong To God — send Link]

No one has power over the spirit to retain the spirit, And no one has power in the day of death. There is no release from that war, And wickedness will not deliver those who are given to it.

—Ecclesiastes 8:8

I call heaven and earth as witnesses today against you, that I have set before you life and death, blessing and cursing; therefore choose life, that both you and your descendants may live; that you may love the LORD your God, that you may obey His voice, and that you may cling to Him, for He is your life and the length of your days; and that you may dwell in the land which the LORD swore to your fathers, to Abraham, Isaac, and Jacob, to give them.

—Deuteronomy 30:19-20

And he said to me, "Who are you?" So I answered him, "I am an Amalekite." He said to me again, "Please stand over me and kill me, for anguish has come upon me, but my life still remains in me." So I stood over him and killed him, because I was sure that he could not live after he had fallen. And I took the crown that was on his head and the bracelet that was on his arm, and have brought them here to my lord." Therefore David took hold of his own clothes and tore them, and so did all the men who were with him. And they mourned and wept and fasted until evening for Saul and for Jonathan his son, for the people of the LORD and for the house of Israel, because they had fallen by the sword. Then David said to the young man who told him, "Where are you from?" And he answered, "I am the son of an alien, an Amalekite." So David said to him, "How was it you were not afraid to put forth your hand to destroy the LORD's anointed?" Then David called one of the young men and said, "Go near, and execute him!" And he struck him so that he died. So David said to him, "Your blood is on your own head, for your own mouth has testified against you, saying, 'I have killed the LORD's anointed.'"

—2 Samuel 1:8-16

The Lord is good to those who wait for Him, to the soul who seeks him. Let him sit alone in silence when it is laid on him; let him put his mouth in the dust—there may yet be hope... though the Lord cause grief, he will have compassion according to the abundance of that steadfast love.

—Lamentations 3:25-32

For this is a gracious thing, when, mindful of God one endures sorrows while suffering unjustly... For to this you have been called, because Christ also suffered for you, leaving you an example, so that you might follow in his steps... When he suffered, he did not threaten, but continued entrusting himself to him who judges justly. He himself bore our sins in his body on the tree, that we might die to sin and live to righteousness. By his wounds you have been healed.

—1 Peter 2: 18-24

Out of the anguish of his soul he shall see light, and be satisfied.

—Isaiah 53:11

For we were so utterly burdened beyond our strength that we despaired of life itself. Indeed we felt that we had received the sentence of death. But that was to make us rely not on ourselves but on God who raises the dead. He delivered us from such a deadly peril, and he will deliver us. On him we have set our hope that he will deliver us again.

—2 Corinthians 1:8-10

And the God of all grace, who called you to his eternal glory in Christ, after you have suffered a little while, will himself restore you and make you strong, firm and steadfast.

—1 Peter 5:10

Therefore, since we have been justified by faith, we have peace with God through our Lord Jesus Christ. Through him we have also obtained access by faith into this grace in which we stand, and we rejoice in hope of the glory of God. More than that, we rejoice in our sufferings, knowing that suffering produces endurance, and endurance produces character, and character produces hope, and hope does not put us to shame, because God's love has been poured into our hearts through the Holy Spirit who has been given to us.

—Romans 5:1-5

The Spirit himself bears witness with our spirit that we are children of God, and if children, then heirs—heirs of God and fellow heirs with Christ, provided we suffer with him in order that we may also be glorified with him.

—Romans 8:16-17

Readings:

To preserve one's life is a duty.

—Emmanuel Kant

Against themselves men may be violent,
And their own lives or their own goods destroy;
So they in the second ring in vain repent.
Who rob themselves of your world, or make a toy
Of fortune, gambling and wasting away their purse,
And turn to weeping what was meant for joy.

—Dante, *Inferno* (Canto XI: 40-45)

The laws against [euthanasia and suicide] reflect the historic principle of the sanctity/inviolability of innocent human life, a principle which has been enshrined for centuries in Western criminal law and for over two thousand years (since the Hippocratic Oath) in Western medical ethics. Our laws and medical ethics have long held that it is a grave wrong for doctors intentionally to kill patients, even at their request. Life is a basic good, with intrinsic and ineradicable value. The value of the patient's life does not depend on the patient's subjective appreciation of it. The fact that a patient may have lost sight of the value of his or her life, through depression or other cause, is no warrant for endorsing that tragically misguided judgment and for assisting that patient to end his or her life. Doctors should no more grant patients' requests for a lethal dose than they should help them jump off a bridge.

—John Keown

Reason and freedom are valued in the Biblical account of human nature. But in the modern, Enlightenment account that has shaped our political institutions and much of our thinking about the contours of caring for one another, reason and freedom are pretty much all there is to a person rightly so called. The modern picture of the human cannot account for our nature as embodied spirits created for and constituted by relationships of love.

—Ken Myers

From a moral vantage point, it can be, though it will not always be, permissible to decline treatment—even potentially life-saving treatment—when one's reason for declining the treatment is something other than the belief that one's life, or the life of the person for whom one is making a decision, lacks sufficient value to be worth living. What we must avoid, always and everywhere, is yielding to the temptation to regard some human lives, or the lives of human beings in certain conditions, as lives unworthy of life. Any society that supposes that there is such a category has deeply morally compromised itself. As Leon Kass recently reminded us in a powerful address at the Holocaust Museum, it was supposedly enlightened and progressive German academics and medical people who put their nation on the road to shame more than a decade before the Nazis rose to power by promoting a doctrine of eugenics based precisely on the proposition that the lives of some human beings—such as the severely retarded—are unworthy of life.

—Professor Robert P. George

Like most people who face death, [Donna] White had three fears: she didn't want to die in pain, she didn't want to die alone, and she didn't want to bring great financial or emotional cost to her family. The only solution to these fears that she knew of was suicide. While searching for a doctor to provide her with the deadly dose, White found a better solution: hospice.

Like 250,000 other terminally ill Americans each year, Donna White found in hospice care the solution to her three driving fears. She would not have to die in pain, because a hospice nurse who specializes in pain relief joined with her doctor to find a more effective combination of drugs to minimize the pain and taught White how to control the amount of drugs she needed. "Once they got my pain under control, I started thinking with my heart," White says. She wouldn't have to die alone, because the hospice concept is built around an integrated support network involving family, friends, medical and spiritual assistance. Finally, she wouldn't bring great financial or emotional loss to her family, because hospice care is considerably less expensive than hospital care, with whatever costs that are not paid by Medicaid underwritten by outside sources. The integrated support of family and friends to the dying process, plus subsequent bereavement counseling, gave White assurance that the emotional cost would also be lessened by the hospice approach.

There are now almost 2000 hospices throughout the United States. As the nation debates issues surrounding health care and costs, euthanasia and assisted suicide, and the patient's right to autonomy in determining the extent to which aggressive curative therapy should be administered, only one approach adequately resolves the issues involved: hospice. As ABC's medical editor Dr. Timothy Johnson, also an ordained clergyman, says, "We should be doing far more in our health-care system to develop and support local hospices. If hospices were geographically and financially available, I believe that the person considering suicide would prefer the hospice. In fact, if we did an adequate job of providing such care, the issue of physician-assisted suicide would largely disappear." If it is going to faithfully care for the dying, the church must actively promote and support hospice.

—Rev. Randall E. Otto, Ph.D.

We must be wary of those who are too willing to end the lives of the elderly and the ill. If we ever decide that a poor quality of life justifies ending that life, we have taken a step down a slippery slope that places all of us in danger. There is a difference between allowing nature to take its course and actively assisting death. The call for euthanasia surfaces in our society periodically, as it is doing now under the guise of "death with dignity" or assisted suicide. Euthanasia is a concept, it seems to me, that is in direct conflict with a religious and ethical tradition in which the human race is presented with "a blessing and a curse, life and death," and we are instructed "...therefore, to choose life." I believe "euthanasia" lies outside the commonly held life-centered values of the West and cannot be allowed without incurring great social and personal tragedy. This is not merely an intellectual conundrum. This issue involves actual human beings at risk....

—Dr. C. Everett Koop, M.D.

I will prescribe regimens for the good of my patients according to my ability and my judgment and never do harm to anyone. I will not give a lethal drug to anyone if I am asked, nor will I advise such a plan; and similarly I will not give a woman a pessary to cause an abortion.

—The original Hippocratic Oath

Commentary and Questions:

Many students of American politics trace the beginning of the reversing of the GOP tide that rolled in 2002 and 2004 to the controversy surrounding the sad story of Terri Schiavo, who died on March 31, 2005. The facts of Ms. Schiavo's case are too complicated for retelling here, but the Congressional Republicans attempted to force judicial reconsideration of the decision by her husband to remove life-sustaining nutrition from Terri Schiavo over the objections of her parents. Courts rebuffed this attempt and Terri Schiavo died after a long period of being denied food and water.

Public opinion polling showed that the public rebelled at the attempt to intervene in the proceedings, and Congressional Republicans bore the brunt of the displeasure. Many observers concluded that the politicians were motivated by a desire to please the "religious right" and not by principle. Even those willing to accept the protests of those leading the legal intervention that they were motivated by a commitment to the sanctity of life thought the effort extremely ill-argued.

The case of Terri Schiavo touched off such enormous controversy and triggered such deep emotions because it involved a nightmare that many Americans have lived and many others fear—the long, painful illness and death of a loved one. The difficulty of such circumstances remains vivid in the memories of all involved, and thus the discussions around such issues are never academic, and are almost always colored by the real-life suffering of those who have lived through such episodes.

Very, very few human beings rejoice in the suffering of others as they approach the end of their earthly lives. The vast majority of people wish that the suffering that often accompanies death be eased. From this common viewpoint spring two very different points of view: That caregivers and doctors should do all that they can to ease suffering short of expediting death and, by sharp contrast, that caregivers and doctors be allowed to expedite death so as to end suffering. The latter practice is euthanasia, and it is commonly practiced with the animals people love, but very rarely practiced—at least openly—with regard to human beings.

The Nazis practiced euthanasia, and the general revulsion at all the crimes of the Nazis led to a widespread refusal to countenance discussions of the practice until recent decades. But the practice is now legal in many states in Europe and forms of it—"physician-assisted suicide," for example—are legal in two states in the United States, Washington and Oregon. Every high-profile case of prolonged suffering in what proponents of euthanasia call a "vegetative state" reignites the debate over what is the humane course of action. Millions of Americans have executed legal documents directing their loved ones to take no extraordinary measures to keep them alive in the event of a terrible injury that robs them of their ability to stay alive without mechanical or intravenous devices.

Christian thought flows across a broad spectrum here, but there is a clear divide between secular humanists and the devout on this issue. The former camp contains some outspoken advocates of expediting the end of life, and for a variety of reasons. Among the deeply devout, the idea of preempting God's plan, even when that plan includes immense suffering, is out of the question.

This is not the place for the debate about the myriad of issues surrounding euthanasia, but rather for a discussion of whether you think God cares about this, and if so, His disposition.

Roman Catholic teaching is quite clear, and the agony of a long dying—lived out in world view in the last days of John Paul II—is not to be preempted by quick dispatch from a doctor or caregiver. In 1980, the Vatican's Sacred Congregation for the Doctrine of the Faith issued a "Declaration on Euthanasia," which declared in unequivocal terms:

By euthanasia is understood an action or an omission which of itself or by intention causes death, in order that all suffering may in this way be eliminated. Euthanasia's terms of reference, therefore, are to be found in the intention of the will and in the methods used.

It is necessary to state firmly once more that nothing and no one can in any way permit the killing of an innocent human being, whether a fetus or an embryo, an infant or an adult, an old person, or one suffering from an incurable disease, or a person who is dying. Furthermore, no one is permitted to ask for this act of killing, either for himself or herself or for another person entrusted to his or her care, nor can he or she consent to it, either explicitly or implicitly. nor can any authority legitimately recommend or permit such an action. For it is a question of the violation of the divine law, an offense against the dignity of the human person, a crime against life, and an attack on humanity.

It may happen that, by reason of prolonged and barely tolerable pain, for deeply personal or other reasons, people may be led to believe that they can legitimately ask for death or obtain it for others. Although in these cases the guilt of the individual may be reduced or completely absent, nevertheless the error of judgment into which the conscience falls, perhaps in good faith, does not change the nature of this act of killing, which will always be in itself something to be rejected. The pleas of gravely ill people who sometimes ask for death are not to be understood as implying a true desire for euthanasia; in fact, it is almost always a case of an anguished plea for help and love. What a sick person needs, besides medical care, is love, the human and supernatural warmth with which the sick person can and ought to be surrounded by all those close to him or her, parents and children, doctors and nurses.

This is a stern and straightforward teaching that seeks to prevent the slow erosion of the safety a bright line rule provides the dying. Many legislatures also concern themselves with bright line rules for fear that overzealous relatives and heirs will want to find a way of getting rid of the burden of an aged or dying relative. Because there are bad people in the world who would prefer their own convenience (or an increase in their own wealth) to the care of a dying parent or relative, governments have to concern themselves with protecting the vulnerable. Too often the unscrupulous want to push granny from the train. And experts opposed to euthanasia also worry that the depressed and weary will move to end their suffering rather than cure their illness.

In the two states—Oregon and Washington—where physician-assisted suicide is available, the protections against abuse are extremely thin. Rita Marker is an attorney and executive director of The International Task Force on Euthanasia and Assisted Suicide, and she did an analysis of the "protections" provided for the American Thinker blog of September 14, 2008:

> *The Oregon law's safeguards are equally problematic. They contain enough loopholes to drive a hearse through them. The safeguards certainly do have the appearance of being protective. They deal with requests for assisted suicide, family notification, and counseling or psychological evaluation. However, those safeguards are about as protective as the emperor's new clothes:*
>
> - *The oral requests, which must be separated by fifteen days, do not need to be witnessed. In fact, they don't even have to be made in person. They could be made by phone—even left on the physician's answering device. The written request must*

be witnessed, but it could be mailed or faxed to the doctor.

- The law states that the physician is to "recommend that the patient notify next of kin," but family notification is not required. It is entirely possible that the first time family members find out that a loved one was contemplating suicide could be after the death has occurred.

- Doctors can facilitate the suicides of mentally-ill or depressed patients without any prior counseling being provided. A psychiatric evaluation is required only if the physician believes that the mental illness or depression is causing impaired judgment. According to Oregon's latest official report, not one patient who died after taking the lethal drugs was referred for counseling prior to being given the prescription.

Additionally troubling are omissions in both Oregon's law and the Washington proposal. For instance, doctor shopping is not prohibited. If one physician refuses to prescribe assisted suicide because, for example, the patient is not competent to make an informed death request, that patient or a family member can go from doctor to doctor until finding one who will write the prescription.

Moreover, neither Oregon's law nor Washington's proposal has any type of protection for the patient once the prescription is written. While the requests for assisted suicide are to be made knowingly and voluntarily, there is no provision that the patient must knowingly and voluntarily take the lethal drugs. Dr. Katrina Hedberg, the lead author of most of Oregon's official reports, acknowledged that there is no assessment of patients after the prescribing is completed. She said that the "law itself only provides for writing the prescription, not what happens afterwards."

This is an unpleasant subject, and the prospect of our own deaths or the deaths of those we love often lead us to turn away from the conversation about how best to deal with end-of-life issues. But as the number of elderly grow and the costs of their care skyrocket, the pressure to increase the availability of legal life-ending options will increase. Already the California Democratic Party called for physician-assisted suicide to be part of their state platform. (The national Democratic Party's platform is silent on the subject.) The entire ideology of the left, however, moves toward the idea that human life can be ended when its "quality" is compromised—a necessary and logical extension of late-term abortion theory even as it is of stem cell research on human embryos. Once any human life becomes less than sacred, the utility of all human life becomes a matter for debate and majoritarian conclusions.

The question for this week is whether you agree with that last paragraph: Is the Democratic Party on a path that will inevitably oblige it to embrace assisted suicide as an option that should be available to all Americans? The Washington and Oregon laws were enacted via direct initiative. Who do you think voted for them? People of faith or secularists? Liberals or conservatives? And does the issue really matter?

See Notes for current
Rep & Dem position

119

Week 19:
National Security, Part 2:
How Much Defense Spending Is Enough?

Scripture:

The LORD is a man of war; The LORD is His name.

—Exodus 15:3

Blessed are the peacemakers, For they shall be called sons of God.

—Matthew 5:9

Readings:

History teaches that wars begin when governments believe the price of aggression is cheap. To keep the peace, we and our allies must be strong enough to convince any potential aggressor that war could bring no benefit, only disaster.

—Ronald Reagan

The great and **chief end**, therefore, of men's uniting into commonwealths, and putting themselves under government, **is the preservation of their property**.

—John Locke

Commentary and Questions:

The United States spends a lot on its military. The Pentagon's budget for 2009 is $487.7 billion dollars, about a 6% hike over 2008's budget. That money pays for a 532,400-member Army;

194,000 Marines; 325,300 men and women in the Navy; and 316,771 members in the Air Force.

All of these men and women have to be paid, and they and their families need medical care as well. They got a 3.9% pay hike in the most recent budget, which few people would begrudge them, and they deserve more. The machines they use are expensive. $3.1 billion dollars will be spent in 2009 to buy 20 F/A-22 "Raptor" fighters. One new destroyer costs $2.6 billion; one new "Virginia"-class sub costs $3.6 billion. Helicopters are relatively cheap: sixty-three Blackhawks will cost the government $1.1 billion.

You get the picture. America has the most powerful military in the world, and that costs—a lot. Many social activists complain about this level of spending and argue that if the U.S. reallocated the money, the funds could help end global malnutrition or disease, or could be used at home to improve schools or healthcare.

The first question, though, asks not how much or what else, but whether we need a military at all, and if so, how to figure out how much to spend on it. Many thousands of experts spend their entire lives as analysts of the Pentagon's budgets, personnel, plans, and armaments. No one with an ounce of common sense should begin a conversation about defense spending with statements of how much needs to be added or deducted from the Pentagon's budget, unless such statements are tethered to serious analysis of where the specific changes are coming from and their short, medium, and long-term impacts on preparedness.

Here's one set of facts you need to know. Gross Domestic Product, or "GDP," is the sum of the value of everything made in the U.S. in any given year. A budget of 10% of GDP means that, as a country, we are spending 10% of our annual wealth on something. Over the past 45 years—from 1962 forward— the country has spent, on average, 5.5% of its GDP on the military. The percentage was much higher during the height of

* 2018 — 649 Billion/3.2% of GDP

the Cold War with the Soviets. We spent about 9.3% of GDP on defense in 1962, and 9.8% in 1968 before a long decline in defense spending as a percentage of GDP began. By 2001, the first year of George W. Bush's two terms in office, and the year of 9/11, defense spending had fallen to 3% of GDP. When President Bush left office in 2009, the Pentagon's budget had climbed back to 4% of GDP.

That's right, just 4%. 4% of the wealth of a country as wealthy as ours is an enormous amount of money, but it is much less a percentage of our wealth devoted to our national security than in years past.

Republicans tend to want to increase defense spending. Democrats tend to want to decrease it. President Obama's transition team indicated it will look for "savings" in the defense budget and expects to reduce the overall total of spending in next year's budget, which the new administration will submit in early 2009 and which Congress will pass in the fall. Only when the budget is passed will we know whether or not the historical tendencies of the Democrats will emerge and defense spending will fall as a result. We live in a very dangerous world, and perhaps the memory of 9/11 will prevent the traditional opponents of defense spending from winning the major cuts they desire.

Do you think 4% is too much or not enough? Do you think the average of the last forty-five years of 5.5% ought to be a target to build to or an anachronism of a long-departed age that needs to be discarded? Can a Christian accept such huge expenditures on weapons and military personnel as a prudent necessity? Much depends on your view of defense spending as a deterrent. Does our huge military establishment hold back the world's evildoers from doing more evil than they already do? Or does it provoke them? Could we beat our swords into plowshares? Or was Ronald Reagan right: More peace is achieved by providing our country with an overwhelming edge that keeps aggressive nations in check. And who do you trust to decide such questions?

We have one great experiment in unilateral disarmament—the appeasement and disarmament policies of Great Britain and France of the 1930s, which those nations adopted in an attempt to persuade Hitler's Germany away from its path of aggression and rearmament. The best book on this subject is William Manchester's *Alone*, which is the second volume of a projected three-volume set on the life of Winston Churchill, which Manchester was never able to finish. *Alone* covers what historians call Churchill's "wilderness years," the years when he was a shunned figure in the British parliament, rising from his seat again and again to warn that Hitler could not be appeased and that British defense spending had dropped to provocatively low levels, especially with regard to the number of planes and pilots that would be needed to defend the British Isles when war came.

Churchill's rhetoric and Hitler's unstoppable aggression eventually awoke England, and England turned to the production of planes just in time to have available the bare number necessary to win the famed Battle of Britain, which raged in the skies over the country from July to October of 1940, when at the cost of 1,023 planes, the Royal Air Force turned back Hitler's Luftwaffe's deadly assault. Had the Luftwaffe succeeded in destroying the British air force, the cross-channel invasion almost certainly would have proceeded and World War II would have been lost, with all the drastic consequences for humanity that a long period of Nazi rule would have meant. That did not happen because Churchill pressed for and eventually woke his country to the peril of cutting defense spending for whatever reason and no matter how difficult the economic times.

Does that argument about deterrence persuade you, and if it is true that strong defenses are indeed the first ingredient for lasting peace, how should a Christian evaluate a politician's votes and record on defense spending?

Week 20:
National Security, Part 3:
Afghanistan, Iraq, Darfur and Rwanda:
When Should the U.S. Invade?

Scripture:

Thus says the LORD: "Go down to the house of the king of Judah, and there speak this word, and say, 'Hear the word of the LORD, O king of Judah, you who sit on the throne of David, you and your servants and your people who enter these gates!' Thus says the LORD: 'Execute judgment and righteousness, and deliver the plundered out of the hand of the oppressor. Do no wrong and do no violence to the stranger, the fatherless, or the widow, nor shed innocent blood in this place.'"

—Jeremiah 22:1-3

To do righteousness and justice Is more acceptable to the LORD than sacrifice.

—Proverbs 21:3

For You will save the humble people, But will bring down haughty looks.

—Psalm 18:27

Readings:

There is also a grave risk in raising the specter of genocide to galvanize a global response to the human rights abuses in Darfur—the international community may be less inclined to react to serious abuses that don't rise to the level of genocide. This could be truly tragic because the only way to prevent genocide is to act at the first sign of threats to civilians. Of the many tragedies of Darfur, one is that it had to be mislabeled a genocide before politicians and activists were stirred to respond.

—Michael Clough

Hundreds of millions of poor people in the developing world today are suffering under an epidemic of violence—domestic abuse, sexual violence, slavery, illegal detention, police abuse, land seizures, and extortion. In their moment of greatest need, Nagaraj and Elisabeth and these millions of others are not crying out for a sermon or food or medicine or housing or microloans. In due course, they may. But right now, they are crying out for someone to restrain the hand of the oppressor. They are crying out for the ministry of justice. You can give all kinds of goods and services to the poor in the name of Christ—but if you have not restrained the hand of the oppressor from simply taking these things away, you have not done much that is significant or sustainable.

—Gary Haugen

Commentary and Questions:

America has this enormous military that can, in fact, topple any non-nuclear regime in the world at some terrible cost in American casualties, but with almost certain success. The U.S. can thus be safely said to possess the ability to remove every pitiless dictator on the globe who does not possess nuclear weapons. (The U.S. could also topple such thugs as North Korea's Kim Jong-il, but at so terrible a cost in the lives of South Koreans and perhaps Japanese that very few people ever think of preemptive strikes on the certainly evil and perhaps insane ruler of the world's most repressive regime. The same inability to act will be true of Iran if the radical mullahs of that country achieve their ambitions.)

At present there are numerous regimes that are brutally repressive at work in the world. Two—the Sudanese government, which allows the terrors of Darfur to proceed, and Robert Mugabe's regime in Zimbabwe—have earned global condemnation for their murderous despotisms.

Since the genocide began in the Darfur region of Sudan, the Sudanese military and the "Janjaweed" militias supported by the Sudanese government have spread terror that has, according to the United Nations, resulted in more than 300,000 deaths. The general objective of the terror campaign is to drive black Africans from their farms and homes so that the land can be taken by the Arab tribes of the county, though some of the victims have themselves been Arab.

In Zimbabwe, the toll of the despotic Mugabe has been more difficult to total because he has been so long in power. The country's economy completely collapsed years ago, and average life expectancy has plummeted from sixty years to thirty-seven years in the past two decades. Mugabe stole the recent election and remains indifferent to the international condemnation heaped upon him.

Both Zimbabwe and Darfur pale in comparison to the genocide that swept Rwanda in 1994, when at least a half million (some estimates go as high as a million) of the country's Tutsis were massacred by the country's Hutu-dominated militias. And who knows how many have perished at the hands of the thugs who run Myanmar, formerly known as Burma. The military junta that seized power in 1962 has ruled ruthlessly since, even refusing international aid when Cyclone Nargis devastated the country in 2008. Estimates of 130,000 deaths may be low and we will never know how many lives could have been saved if the police state had allowed the world to come to its aid.

Over and over again, the world sees terrible regimes run by ruthless killers murder, imprison, starve, and destroy, and all that follows is condemning resolutions from the United Nations. Expressions of regret that follow later—Bill Clinton famously apologized in the Rwandan capital of Kigali in 1998 for not having done enough to stop the killing—do nothing to restore shattered lives and families, and the suffering of the maimed and dead is not in any way lessened by even the most sincere regret.

How ought the U.S. to act vis-à-vis such monsters, and once a rule of action is decided upon, which political party is most likely to support such a rule?

Bill Clinton intervened in Kosovo; George W. Bush in Iraq. Both actions brought an end to bloody conflicts. Bill Clinton's dispatch of the military to Haiti in the fall of 1994—led to no lasting change in the miserable conditions of the nation. Though the Taliban has been toppled by the American-led coalition that invaded Afghanistan in the aftermath of the attack on the U.S. of September 11, 2001, and conditions there are better than under the fanatical extremists of the Taliban. The country is still wracked by violence and faces a unsteady future of ongoing war with local chieftains and a reconstituted Pakistan-based Taliban. In short, invasions don't always work though they almost always can topple the existing regime and force such dictators and their supporters to flee into the countryside to fight another day.

This is the reality of discussions about America's use of force. For Christians, though, it is the difficulty of the expeditions and the necessary loss of American lives; they will always provide reasons enough to turn eyes away from slaughters and repressions on the scale of those noted above.

Isn't there an obligation to do the best we can even at the enormous cost such expeditions entail? Should we act in Darfur and Zimbabwe, Haiti and Burma, and if so, where first? Where the killing is the most extreme? Where we can most easily achieve the removal of the dictator? Only when the U.N. accords us the green light? And which party has the better record of effectively stopping the rampages of dictators?

Week 21:
National Security, Part 4:
Does Christ Condemn Waterboarding?

Scripture:

So his fellow servant fell down at his feet and begged him, saying, "Have patience with me, and I will pay you all." And he would not, but went and threw him into prison till he should pay the debt. So when his fellow servants saw what had been done, they were very grieved, and came and told their master all that had been done. Then his master, after he had called him, said to him, "You wicked servant! I forgave you all that debt because you begged me. Should you not also have had compassion on your fellow servant, just as I had pity on you?" And his master was angry, and delivered him to the torturers until he should pay all that was due to him.

So My heavenly Father also will do to you if each of you, from his heart, does not forgive his brother his trespasses.

—Matthew 18:29-35

And suddenly they cried out, saying, "What have we to do with You, Jesus, You Son of God? Have You come here to torment us before the time?"

—Matthew 8:29

Readings:

War is an art and as such is not susceptible of explanation by fixed formula.

—General George Patton, Jr.

129

May God have mercy upon my enemies, because I won't.

—General George Patton, Jr.

The point is that terrorism has consequences beyond life and property. It requires a tightening of liberty no one desires. The prevention of terrorism prevents the need, real or perceived, for further tightening.

—Jonah Goldberg, December 14, 2007

You probably don't think I could force this towel down your throat, but trust me I can. All the way. Except that I'd hold onto this little bit at the end. When your stomach starts to digest the towel, I pull it out. Taking your stomach lining with it. Most people probably take about a week to die. It's very painful.

—Jack Bauer

I'm done talking with you, you understand me? You've read my file. The first thing I'm going to do is take out your right eye, and then I'm gonna move over and take out your left, and then I'm going to cut you. I'm gonna keep cutting you until you give me the information that I need. Do you understand me? So for the last time, where is the nerve gas?

—Jack Bauer

Commentary and Questions:

As a talk show host, I could throw the subject of the use of torture out there on any slow news day and instantly fill the board with callers adamant about both sides of the issue. Because I have discussed the subject with experts on many occasions over the years, here is a fair summary of the debate.

Interrogation is a necessity in any war as the enemy—whether lawful or unlawful combatants, uniformed military, or terrorists without regular insignia or discipline—has information we need to prevent the death of our own troops or our own people, or the troops and people of our allies. Interrogation has yielded enormously valuable, life-saving information in the war which most people date to September 11, 2001.

There is a spectrum of interrogation techniques that range from patient, skilled questioning over many months and years, to horrifically brutal and sadistic torture we most commonly associate with the Nazis. The United States has used a range of techniques that included "waterboarding," which simulates drowning, as well as prolonged periods of standing and exposure to cold and loud music, as well as extended periods of sleep deprivation.

Some legal experts believe some of these "enhanced interrogation techniques" amount to torture and believe it to be illegal and those who authorize and carry out these techniques to be criminals. Other legal experts disagree. Most experts agree that most torture produces unreliable information, as the person subjected to torture will provide made-up information just to make the pain stop.

Many U.S. allies in the war against terror are suspected of routinely using torture on their prisoners. The U.S., since the time of the first President Bush and President Clinton, have sent terrorism suspects to countries suspected of using torture, though we have usually obtained agreements with the country receiving the suspect that torture would not be used. Many suspect these agreements are routinely broken.

Terrorism is a fact of modern life, and though at this writing the U.S. has not been subjected to another major terror attack after 9/11, the world's headlines have all too often carried the details of terrible attacks elsewhere. If you'd like to be depressed, type "List of Terrorist Incidents" into Wikipedia, and you will almost certainly be surprised by the number of incidents that occur around the globe every month. Americans only hear of the highest-profile or most lurid of them—the Mumbai coordinated assaults, the Madrid train station bombing, the London subway bombing, the Beslan school massacre, the Bali nightclub bombing, to name just five.

Every day terrorists plot their mayhem. When the U.S. military or intelligence agencies capture a terrorist, the information that can be gained from them can save many lives, and prevent perhaps another 9/11 or an even worse attack.

Television's Jack Bauer is quoted above; he is a fictional counter-terrorism agent who has, through his very successful virtual career, routinely resorted to torture of the sort that is clearly illegal. Bauer's resort to violence is matched and usually exceeded by fiction's Mitch Rapp, the hero of the best-selling Vince Flynn-authored novels. Almost every one of Flynn's Rapp novels involves Rapp using physical punishment to extract crucial information, in one instance, to prevent the detonation of a nuclear device in the nation's capitol.

This is where *Washington Post* columnist Charles Krauthammer picks up the argument in an article written in 2005 for *The Weekly Standard*:

> Here the issue of torture gets complicated and the easy pieties don't so easily apply. Let's take the textbook case. Ethics 101: A terrorist has planted a nuclear bomb in New York City. It will go off in one hour. A million people will die. You capture the terrorist. He knows where it is. He's not talking.
>
> Question: If you have the slightest belief that hanging this man by his thumbs will get you the information to save a million people, are you permitted to do it? Now, on most issues regarding torture, I confess tentativeness and uncertainty. But on this issue, there can be no uncertainty: Not only is it permissible to hang this miscreant by his thumbs. It is a moral duty.

Yes, you say, but that's an extreme and very hypothetical case. Well, not as hypothetical as you think. Sure, the (nuclear) scale is hypothetical, but in the age of the car-and suicide-bomber, terrorists are often captured who have just set a car bomb to go off or sent a suicide bomber out to a coffee shop, and you only have minutes to find out where the attack is to take place. This "hypothetical" is common enough that the Israelis have a term for precisely that situation: the ticking time bomb problem.

And even if the example I gave were entirely hypothetical, the conclusion—yes, in this case even torture is permissible—is telling because it establishes the principle: Torture is not always impermissible. However rare the cases, there are circumstances in which, by any rational moral calculus, torture not only would be permissible but would be required (to acquire life-saving information). And once you've established the principle, to paraphrase George Bernard Shaw, all that's left to haggle about is the price. In the case of torture, that means that the argument is not whether torture is ever permissible, but when—i.e., under what obviously stringent circumstances: how big, how imminent, how preventable the ticking time bomb.

Krauthammer's concise summary didn't end the argument. It rages still, four years later. It will rage forever. What does a Christian think about this issue that a non-Christian might not, if anything? Would the prospect of saving millions allow a Christian to conduct an interrogation that used waterboarding or other similar techniques? Or does the example of Christ, who Himself was tortured, oblige us to say "never"?

If you agree with Krauthammer's conclusion—"torture is not always impermissible"—then you have only begun the inquiry. "When?" and "for how long?" quickly follow, and we are rolling down the very long slope toward barbarism. As you discuss this today, keep in mind past weeks' discussions of why we needed to have bright lines in the debate over unborn life. The same bright lines and the same demand for the protection of all human life—yes, even those of terrorists—should be at work in this discussion.

If you conclude that the greater good requires the conclusion that "torture is not always impermissible," then keep in mind that Republicans and Democrats divide over this issue sharply, with the latter committed to an absolute bright line against the use of "enhanced interrogation techniques," including waterboarding.

Week 22:
The Problem of Race: Where to Now?

Scripture:

Therefore love the stranger, for you were strangers in the land of Egypt.

—Deuteronomy 10:19

Readings:

You can't say you love God and not love your brother.

—Bill McCartney

Until justice is blind to color, until education is unaware of race, until opportunity is unconcerned with the color of men's skins, emancipation will be a proclamation but not a fact.

—Lyndon B. Johnson

Whoever in prayer can say, "Our Father," acknowledges and should feel the brotherhood of the whole race of mankind.

—Tryon Edwards

Commentary and Questions:

Here is a column I wrote for Townhall.com on the day Barack Obama was inaugurated as president, titled "The Completion":

President Barack Obama's Inaugural Address was much more than a speech, however satisfying and moving it may have been for hundreds of millions of Americans and others across the globe.

And it was much more than a political statement about what is on the agenda for the years 2009 through at least 2012.

Though many will grade the new president's rhetoric, and attempt to glean from it some guide to the term ahead, the significance of the speech has very little to do with its particular giver or its particular content. Its greatest significance is rather that it marks the completion of the repair of the Constitution, which had been flawed in its framing because of its departure from the Declaration that preceded it all those years ago.

The Constitution was flawed because it had to be to give birth to the Union. The repair of that flaw was begun with Lincoln's election and the worst of the pain required by the repair was endured in the Civil War, though the suffering of blacks would continue through the long years of Jim Crow and of course even after the Civil Rights Act of 1964 and the Voting Rights Act of 1965.

But the terrible force of the Declaration's central demand—"that all men are created equal, that they are endowed by their Creator with certain unalienable Rights, that among these are Life, Liberty and the Pursuit of Happiness"—has rolled forward from 1776 until on January 20, 2009, it became embodied in the ascent to the nation's highest office of a black man. What had come into the world as a radical idea birthed by a slaveholder, Jefferson, became real in its most blindingly obvious form in the son of an African being sworn in on Lincoln's own Bible.

Barack and Michelle Obama's personal triumph is extraordinary, but it is also the triumph of an idea for which hundreds and thousands have fought and died over the centuries, and to which hundreds of millions more have been pledged. It is an idea birthed in America but which travels abroad now to the far corners of the world, and the finest moments in the new president's speech were those addressed to the dictators of the world and to the enemies of that idea.

> We will not apologize for our way of life, nor will we waver in its defense, and for those who seek to advance their aims by inducing terror and slaughtering innocents, we say to you now that our spirit is stronger and cannot be broken; you cannot outlast us, and we will defeat you.

President Obama closed his remarks by quoting the father of our country, George Washington, ordinarily an unremarkable borrowing, but in this context, at least a bit surprising, for the great Washington was also a slave-owner, and not one tortured by the institution in the way Jefferson was. Some of my conservative friends thought that the new president was too quick and perfunctory in his recognition of the departing President Bush, and a few more words addressed to him would have indeed been welcomed by the admirers of the 43rd president.

But it was remarkably gracious for the new president to summon the first president to the occasion of the completion of the work of Philadelphia in 1776. This does not mean, of course, that justice is established or that the human condition is closing in on the happiness we believe a perfected world would hold for all.

Only that in one country—the most powerful in all of human history—there is no bar to anyone becoming its chief executive, no exception to the rule that all men and women are indeed created equal.

The rise to the presidency of the first African-American president doesn't solve the problem of racism, because all sin, including the sin of hateful prejudice based on race, isn't going away until the world is redeemed by the return of Christ.

What continues to matter in politics is whether the government should ever use race to inflict penalties or award benefits. By far the most often debated subject in the category of "politics and race" is the use of race to award places in higher education or government contracting—a practice long known as "affirmative action."

Race-based quotas have been illegal in the United States for some years now, and the United States Supreme Court has declared repeatedly that any "hard" quota—such as setting aside a number of admission slots in an incoming medical school class—is unconstitutional and will be struck down. But the court has been willing—by a very narrow margin of five to four votes—to allow race to be used as a "soft" factor in granting admission to college and graduate schools.

This isn't a book about the Supreme Court, but this is an issue near and dear to many hearts, so here is an excerpt from Justice Sandra Day O'Connor's opinion in the 2003 case of *Grutter v. University of Michigan Law School,* which upheld the use of race in selecting the Michigan Law School's class:

> *In order to cultivate a set of leaders with legitimacy in the eyes of the citizenry, it is necessary that the path to leadership be visibly open to talented and qualified individuals of every race and ethnicity. All members of our heterogeneous society must have confidence in the openness and integrity of the educational institutions that provide this training. As we have recognized, law schools cannot be effective in isolation from the individuals and institutions with which the law interacts. Access to legal education (and thus the legal profession) must be inclusive of talented and qualified individuals of every race and ethnicity, so that all*

*members of our heterogeneous society may participate in
the educational institutions that provide the training and
education necessary to succeed in America.*

Justice O'Connor's opinion is much longer than this
excerpt, of course, and her reassuring for accepting the
University of Michigan Law School's program is much more
complex than this single paragraph conveys, but here is a great
divide in American politics: Can fairness to individuals be
sacrificed in order to serve the common good and/or the cause
of a long-discriminated-against group?

The case challenging the admissions policy was brought by
a white woman with excellent grades and fine test scores. She
received no "extra points" for being a woman, so obviously she
didn't compete on a level playing field with minority applicants. Many argue that this is deeply unjust, and that an individual like Barbara Grutter should never be asked to shoulder
the full burden of past discrimination against minorities. They
further argue that race doesn't tell you enough about an appli-
cant to justify preferring them in even a small degree over other
non-minority applicants. Individuals deserve to be treated as
individuals.

Christians played an important role in the Civil Rights
Movement, and of course Dr. Martin Luther King was a pastor,
a Christian preacher in the long line of Christian preachers
demanding justice for the oppressed. He wanted a color-blind
society, but he also knew that racism would persist long after
legal segregation was erased from the law books of the land.

The debate over affirmative action will go on for many
more years, and it sharply divides the Republican Party from
the Democratic Party. If a Republican is in the White House,
he or she will almost certainly appoint justices that strike down
most uses of race in every setting, including admissions to
colleges and universities. A Democratic president, by contrast,
will almost certainly appoint judges who see exceptions to the

Constitution's ban on using race in governmental decision-making when that use is to benefit a long-discriminated-against group.

Where are you in this conversation, and how important an issue is this anyway in a time of war and economic upheaval? Has it figured in the way you have voted in the past? Some states have held elections on initiatives to completely ban affirmative action in their states. How would you vote on such a question and why? And does the election of President Obama signal that the time has arrived where merit truly does triumph over race?

Week 23:
The Islamists and the West: How Great a Threat?

Scripture:

For whoever finds me finds life, And obtains favor from the LORD; But he who sins against me wrongs his own soul; All those who hate me love death.

> —Proverbs 8:35-36

The wicked plots against the just, And gnashes at him with his teeth. The Lord laughs at him, For He sees that his day is coming.

> —Psalm 37:11-13

The future of our civilization does not rest merely on the advance of material wealth and technological prowess; the future of the West turns on the question of whether our spiritual aspirations are noble or base.

> —George Weigel

Islam, we've been told, is related to the Arabic word meaning "peace." This is correct, except that the word means a particular kind of peace. A better translation is "surrender" or "submission." It describes the peace when a vanquished soldier lays down his arms in submission. And so the very name, Islam, has militaristic connotations, and in this lies the root of radical Islam. That root then grows in the soil of the Islamic worldview.

> —Chuck Colson

Commentary and Questions:

In the years since 9/11, I have devoted a great deal of time on my radio show to the issue of the "Islamist threat." This is the threat posed to people of all backgrounds, races, and religions by radical terrorists, both Sunni and Shia. The Islamists believe themselves to be under a religious duty to destroy anyone who does not believe in their understanding of the commands of the Koran. They are religious fanatics, and they will kill for their cause.

As 2008 came to a close, I collected into one book more than thirty interviews I had done with leading experts on Radical Islam, ranging from General David Petraeus and historian Victor Davis Hanson to *New York Times* Baghdad bureau chief and Pulitzer Prize winner John Burns and *New Yorker* writer and Pulitzer Prize winner Lawrence Wright, whose amazing, riveting book, *The Looming Tower*, is basically a genealogy of al-Qaeda. My book, *The War Against the West*, might make an excellent successor to this study if you find yourself intrigued by the issues raised here about the war because the experts I interviewed come from across the whole political spectrum, and their knowledge about the nature of our enemy is vast and deeply disturbing. (The book is available at HughHewiit. com.)

After all these years of study and interviews, I know mostly what we in the United States don't know. As a whole, we are deeply ignorant of Islam generally and of the radical extremists within it specifically. Oh, we know they are out there and we certainly remember the horrors of 9/11. But as the years have gone by and the distance from the drama, pain, and suffering of that day has lengthened, we think less and less about who they are and what they believe, and more and more about the economy or some other issue. Terrorism makes headlines every so often, as we saw two chapters back, but sustained focus on the nature of the enemy is nonexistent, and even great books on the subject languish on bookstore shelves.

Christians have a special obligation to be better informed about this battle because the Islamists have declared again and again that theirs is a war targeting Jews and Christians. One historian of the Crusades, Jonathan Riley-Smith, wrote for *National Review* in 2004 on bin Laden's use of the term "crusader" in his writings. "When Osama bin Laden and his followers refer, as they often do, to crusades and crusaders," Riley-Smith writes, "they are not using language loosely. They are expressing a historical vision, an article of faith that has helped to provide moral justification for the actions of both Arab nationalists and radical Islamists." He continues:

> *Osama bin Laden's militant wing of Islamism is also inspired by a theory of jihad that demands turning inwards to purge Islam of infidels and heretics, renewing individual spirituality and creating a united, triumphant society dedicated to God. This is why Osama appears to be so emotional about infidel penetration, which, he believes, defiles Islam and particularly its holy places:*
>
> > *Our lord, the people of the cross had come with their horses (soldiers) and occupied the land of the two Holy Places (Mecca and Medina) and the Zionist Jews fiddle as they wish with the al-Aqsa mosque.*
> >
> > *The Arabian Peninsula has never—since Allah made it flat, created its desert, and encircled it with seas—been stormed by any forces like the crusader armies, spreading in it like locusts, eating its riches and wiping out its plantations.... For over seven years the United States has been occupying the lands of Islam in the holiest of places, the Arabian Peninsula, plundering its riches,*

dictating to its rulers, humiliating its people, terrorizing its neighbors, and turning its bases in the Peninsula into a spearhead through which to fight the neighboring Muslim peoples.

To be found fighting under the sign of the cross are not only Christians, but also their surrogates, Jews, Marxists and secularists. And Afghanistan has been for decades a theatre of crusading warfare in a world-wide conflict.

This is a battle of Muslims against the global crusaders.... God, who provided us with his support and kept us steadfast until the Soviet Union was defeated, is able to provide us once more with his support to defeat America on the same land and with the same people.

In a war of civilizations, our goal is for our nation to unite in the face of the Christian crusade... This is a recurring war. The original crusade brought Richard (Lionheart) from Britain, Louis from France and Barbarossa from Germany. Today the crusading countries rushed as soon as Bush raised the cross. They accepted the rule of the cross.

It is this radical vision of crusade history which has suddenly and spectacularly forced itself on the outside world. Although merely a fantasy to the West, it finds expression in many Muslim societies. It is said that in mosques in Egypt, the word "crusader" has become a synonym for "Christian." In Indonesia last year, local preachers were referring to the dead at Bali in the same terms.

We are therefore confronted by a dangerous view of the past and of the present, moral as well as historical, shared by both Arab nationalists and Islamists. It has been spreading for a century and nothing has been done *to counter it. Indeed, over and over again, in words and deeds, Westerners have thoughtlessly reinforced many Muslims' belief in it.*

This "radical vision" is not a political movement with which compromise is possible. It is not born out of poverty, but of religious zeal. Osama bin Laden was born into a fabulously wealthy family and many of his followers are very well-educated and could have led lives of accomplishment and economic security. While many recruits to the jihadist cause do come from impoverished regions and countries and do become brainwashed in religious schools that teach little but the Koran, the movement is not a social-political one like the one that birthed the communist revolutionaries who overthrew the tsar, but a profoundly religious one that celebrates martyrdom and the death of civilians.

The political parties in the U.S. are deeply divided on how to wage the war against the Sunni Islamist jihadists of al-Qaeda and the Shia Islamist jihadists of Iran. Republicans generally do not believe there is hope for negotiations or compromise with these radical movements, whether it be al-Qaeda and the Taliban in Afghanistan and Pakistan, Hamas in Gaza, Hezbollah in Lebanon, or the mullahs and Revolutionary Guard in Iran. The harsh realism of George Bush and Donald Rumsfeld was birthed in the tragedy of 9/11, and they were never not aware of our enemies' deeply evil intentions.

Many Democrats, on the other hand, tend to believe that there are negotiated settlements out there waiting to happen with almost everyone (though not al-Qaeda, of course, which will forever remain a pariah in the U.S.). When President Obama was Senator Obama, he famously declared in one debate with Senator Clinton that he would meet and negotiate without precondition with Iran's anti-Semitic president Mahmoud Ahmadinejad, a statement that is consistent with the deeply utopian streak within left-liberalism when it comes to the belief in the power of talking. President Obama took a long time to vigorously condemn the regression in Iran following the stolen election here.

Christians have to ask themselves if their government is taking seriously the ambitions of the Islamist jihadists and if their government is seriously committed to protecting the homeland via an aggressive engagement of the enemy far from our shores. "We fight them over there so we don't have to fight them here" is now a cliché, though in the first few years after 9/11 it made perfect sense to a traumatized nation.

Do you know much about radical Islam? Have you read any books about it, such as Lawrence Wright's *The Looming Tower*? Has your pastor ever preached on the subject? Do you think Republicans and Democrats are different when it comes to assessing this threat, and if so how? And have you ever voted on the basis of a candidate's view about the threat posed by Radical Islam?

Week 24:
How Urgent Are The Days
(and Do You Act Accordingly)?

Scripture:

But know this, that in the last days perilous times will come: For men will be lovers of themselves, lovers of money, boasters, proud, blasphemers, disobedient to parents, unthankful, unholy, unloving, unforgiving, slanderers, without self-control, brutal, despisers of good, traitors, headstrong, haughty, lovers of pleasure rather than lovers of God, having a form of godliness but denying its power. And from such people turn away!

—Timothy 3:1-5

"These things which you see—the days will come in which not one stone shall be left upon another that shall not be thrown down." So they asked Him, saying, "Teacher, but when will these things be? And what sign will there be when these things are about to take place?" And He said: "Take heed that you not be deceived. For many will come in My name, saying, 'I am He,' and, 'The time has drawn near.' Therefore do not go after them."

—Luke 21:6-8

Even if I knew that tomorrow the world would go to pieces, I would still plant my apple tree.

—Martin Luther King, Jr.

Commentary and Questions:

In the nine years since I launched my nationally-syndicated radio show, the country and the world has not lacked for crises. The bombing of the USS Cole occurred just weeks after I began the broadcast, and the campaign of 2000 between George Bush and Al Gore gave way to the months of high stakes recounting and courtroom drama in Florida. The early months of the Bush years saw huge partisan wrangles as Bush pushed for tax cuts and Vermont Senator Jim Jeffords jumped parties and stalled the GOP legislative program—and many of its judicial nominees—for a year and a half. Then came 9/11 and the invasion of Afghanistan. Then came the ultimatums to Saddam, the Bush triumph in the elections of 2002, and the quick toppling of Saddam followed by the long and terrible occupation of Iraq with its toll of American lives and severely wounded soldiers, sailors, airmen, and Marines. No WMDs were found, and a brutal domestic political campaign began that ended with Bush's re-election but a deeply divided country. Then Terri Schiavo, then Katrina, and the wars dragged on in both Afghanistan and Iraq.

The Republicans paid a huge price at the polls in 2006, and the paralysis that followed in D.C. was not eased by the success of the surge in Iraq. The campaign of 2008 was marred by religious bigotry against Mitt Romney and lifted up by the energy of the mobilized millions drawn to politics by Barack Obama. Then another crisis—an oil shock—battered budgets and was followed by the banking crisis and a stock market plunge that left lifetime savings decimated and homes devalued. President Obama took office amid high hopes and monumental problems. Though he had kept America safe from another 9/11, George W. Bush left Washington with approval numbers rivaling Truman's when he left in 1953. Three days after he took the oath of office, and one day after he signed an executive order promising the closing of the Guantanamo prison for terrorists, President Obama was commander-in-chief when a missile strike hit a Pakistani village and killed twenty.

The war goes on in many places around the globe and the economy remains fragile. Oil, which plummeted in price, has begun to rise again, but it is still a declining source of energy. Israel fought another battle with Hamas two-and-a-half years after its inconclusive war with Hezbollah. Russia invaded Georgia and cut gas supplies to Ukraine. China hosted the Olympics but then reeled as the worldwide banking crisis sapped even the Dragon's remarkable economic energy. Al-Qaeda terrorists experimenting with the bubonic plague wiped out forty of their own number. Mexico reeled under the assault of the drug traffickers, and the Mugabe of South America, Hugo Chavez, tightened his despotic grip on the country even as his predecessor in brutality, Fidel Castro, wasted away.

We live in interesting times. We tend to focus on the dramatic reverses, but these years have also seen elections in Afghanistan and Iraq and stability rising in the latter. Libya has completely abandoned its many WMD hopes and the U.S. has disassembled Khaddafi's nuclear, chemical, and biological weapons programs and brought the components back to the U.S. for safe destruction. Tens of thousands of jihadists have been captured and killed. Even the hard-hit stock markets and housing values are still in price ranges that reflect enormous wealth in the U.S. Unemployment is high, but in 1933, it reached more than 70% in Toledo, Ohio, and probably above 25% nationally. It is around 10% at this writing. Times are tough, especially for the unemployed, but the world is very different from 1929 and 1932. Governments have acted, refusing a passive approach.

But Iran is seeking a nuclear bomb—many of them actually. And its senior leaders speak with unbridled hatred of Israel and predict Israel will vanish from the map. Iran brutally repressed its people after the false election of June 2009. Syria was up to no good when Israel intervened and destroyed what is widely understood to have been some sort of a nuclear weapons facility. North Korea continues to brutalize its desperate people and to export WMDs. Pakistan, with its dozens and dozens of nuclear weapons, remains the most unstable of nuclear powers, and China continues to periodically rattle its saber at Taiwan.

The bird flu appears. It goes away. Ebola strikes suddenly in Africa and burns itself out in the quarantined area. The new swine flu appears, panics the world, and then recedes as a threat. Genocide continues in Darfur. The tyrant Mugabe continues to mercilessly oppress Zimbabwe.

What's a Christian to think? Lots of "end-time" folks have sold lots of "end-time" books charting out "end-time" scenarios. Are you among their readers? This is the week to lay your cards on the table. Are you one who sees the end of history approaching?

I am not. I don't believe anyone knows the day or the hour, and I think that every age thinks it is uniquely under siege. Admittedly, the return of the Jews to Israel is one of those events that make you wonder, but step back. Is it really so strange that a historically over-achieving race would find their way back to their roots once the technology of travel and transfer caught up with the reality of global anti-Semitism and of Hitler's genocide?

Still, as Walker Percy once wrote (I am paraphrasing here) the historical reality of the Jews ought to give the non-believer pause. Never did a race have less going for them politically, but their central role in history ought to compel you to ask if their God is the God. Skeptics say some race had to win, and the Jews as a whole are no more special than every human being who won the lottery and outlasted a trillion, zillion other genes is special.

The history of the Jews points us to Scripture, and to God's narrative of our story, and the question should be asked before we get to the closing sprint in this half-year of conversations: Do politics matter at all? Wouldn't we all be better off on our knees and praying rather than organizing and arguing for a better way forward for politics? Or, if the world isn't coming to its end and you believe in Christ, don't you owe the world a lot of effort to make it better? Have you been paying your dues?

Week 25:
Do You Contribute Time, Talent, and Treasure to Politics?

Scripture:

> But his lord answered and said to him, "You wicked and lazy servant, you knew that I reap where I have not sown, and gather where I have not scattered seed."
> —Matthew 25:26

Readings:

> And, sir, when we think of eternity, and of the future consequences of all human conduct, what is there in this life that should make any man contradict the dictates of his conscience, the principles of justice, the laws of religion, and of God?
> —William Wilberforce

> Is it not the great end of religion, and, in particular, the glory of Christianity, to extinguish the malignant passions; to curb the violence, to control the appetites, and to smooth the asperities of man; to make us compassionate and kind, and forgiving one to another; to make us good husbands, good fathers, good friends; and to render us active and useful in the discharge of the relative social and civil duties?
> —William Wilberforce

Commentary and Questions:

Every single day of every single year, millions of Americans are actively involved in politics. They read, correspond, and talk about politics with friends, family, and often complete strangers. They blog, twitter, Facebook, and e-mail their thoughts, and they often attend meetings of groups both large and small. Some serve on the local Republican or Democratic committee or related clubs. Others are involved in particular candidacies. Still others throw themselves into political action committees such as MoveOn.org or the Christian Coalition. Are you among them? If not, have you ever been involved?

Discuss among yourselves what you have done in the past with regard to politics, and why you are doing more or less today. Have the issues grown less important, or more so? Is the country headed in the right direction or the wrong direction? Are the threats to your children's future and that of your grand-children greater or lesser than they were ten years ago?

Non-political activism is a great way to evaluate how committed you are to the future of the country. Are you involved with your church, and if so, how much time and money do you put into it? How about your kids' schools or youth sports? We invest ourselves and our money in things that matter to us, and usually in places where we think we will make a difference. Individuals can and do impact politics. Chances are even one more committed, talented volunteer to the Norm Coleman re-election campaign for the United States Senate in Minnesota would have put Norm over the top and sent him back to Washington rather than comedian-turned-politician Al Franken. That's a huge difference on any number of issues: A center-right Republican replaced by perhaps the most extreme member of the Senate both in terms of left-wing politics and personality. One committed volunteer could have turned that race. Five almost certainly would have.

Lots of elections are decided by very close margins, and more importantly, lots of volunteers across the country turn national races one direction or the other. Political activism has enormous consequences both in the short term and very much so in the long term. So do political contributions. Very few people actually write checks to candidates, but political contributions are the stuff of winning campaigns. A very famous California Democrat named Jesse Unruh remarked many years ago that "Money is the mother's milk of politics," and he was right. EMILY's List, a pro-abortion rights advocacy group, takes its name from the saying "Early Money Is Like Yeast," meaning that early financial support allows promising candidates to get their base of support organized and their campaigns off to great starts.

Discuss in your group if any of you have ever made a contribution to a candidate or a political cause, and if so, why and how much. Ask if anyone has ever hosted a fundraiser in their home, inviting family and friends to meet an aspiring candidate at some level. This is a mark of serious political involvement, the sort of meeting that people organize for things that concern them greatly.

Christians routinely exert themselves on behalf of their churches and the mission work of their churches, but rarely is the same level of commitment or anything remotely approaching that level of commitment displayed regarding politics. This is odd given that religious freedom depends upon the continuation of our government, and the spread of freedom around the globe allows for the gospel to spread more easily. Of course, the gospel does not require political freedom to spread. The house church movement in China is one example of where the power of the gospel has overcome even severe restrictions on its preaching.

But political freedom greatly advantages the preaching of the Good News. There is no doubt that more opportunities to hear the gospel would follow a great expansion of freedom in many countries. To maintain vibrant religious freedom in the United States and to assure its maintenance and spread across the globe, Christians must work to preserve and extend that freedom. And that means political involvement. That means political contributions. That means as much of yourself in politics as in anything else for which you care deeply and which will certainly impact you, your family, and your country.

Finding a way to make a significant contribution to political life isn't hard to do, though there are lots of ways to waste time, talent, and treasure. If you are convicted of the need to become involved in a serious way, ask a few people already involved for suggestions. Then choose wisely and begin.

Week 26:
Do You Have The Courage To Lead?
Does Your Pastor? Does Your Church?

Scriptures:

Be strong and of good courage, do not fear nor be afraid of them; for the LORD your God, He is the One who goes with you. He will not leave you nor forsake you.

—Deuteronomy 31:6

Then Daniel, whose name *was* Belteshazzar, was astonished for a time, and his thoughts troubled him. *So* the king spoke, and said, "Belteshazzar, do not let the dream or its interpretation trouble you."

Belteshazzar answered and said, "My lord, *may* the dream concern those who hate you, and its interpretation concern your enemies!

"The tree that you saw, which grew and became strong, whose height reached to the heavens and which *could be seen* by all the earth, whose leaves *were* lovely and its fruit abundant, in which *was* food for all, under which the beasts of the field dwelt, and in whose branches the birds of the heaven had their home—it *is* you, O king, who have grown and become strong; for your greatness has grown and reaches to the heavens, and your dominion to the end of the earth.

"And inasmuch as the king saw a watcher, a holy one, coming down from heaven and saying, 'Chop down the tree and destroy it, but leave its stump and roots in the earth, *bound* with a band of iron and bronze in the tender grass of the field; let it be wet with the dew of heaven, and let him graze with the beasts of the field, till seven times pass over him'; this is the interpretation, O king, and this is the decree of the Most High, which has come upon my lord the king: They shall drive you from men, your dwelling shall be with the beasts of the field, and they shall make you eat grass like oxen. They shall wet you with the dew of heaven, and seven times shall pass over you, till you know that the Most High rules in the kingdom of men, and gives it to whomever He chooses.

"And inasmuch as they gave the command to leave the stump *and* roots of the tree, your kingdom shall be assured to you, after you come to know that Heaven rules. Therefore, O king, let my advice be acceptable to you; break off your sins by *being* righteous, and your iniquities by showing mercy to *the* poor. Perhaps there may be a lengthening of your prosperity."

All *this* came upon King Nebuchadnezzar. At the end of the twelve months he was walking about the royal palace of Babylon. The king spoke, saying, "Is not this great Babylon, that I have built for a royal dwelling by my mighty power and for the honor of my majesty?"

While the word *was still* in the king's mouth, a voice fell from heaven: "King Nebuchadnezzar, to you it is spoken: the kingdom has departed from you! And they shall drive you from men, and your dwelling *shall be* with the beasts of the field. They shall make you eat grass like oxen; and seven times shall pass over you, until you know that the Most High rules in the kingdom of men, and gives it to whomever He chooses."

That very hour the word was fulfilled concerning Nebuchadnezzar; he was driven from men and ate grass like oxen; his body was wet with the dew of heaven till his hair had grown like eagles' *feathers* and his nails like birds' *claws.*

And at the end of the time I, Nebuchadnezzar, lifted my eyes to heaven, and my understanding returned to me; and I blessed the Most High and praised and honored Him who lives forever:

For His dominion *is* an everlasting dominion,
And His kingdom *is* from generation to
    generation.
All the inhabitants of the earth *are* reputed as
    nothing;
He does according to His will in the army of
    heaven.
And *among* the inhabitants of the earth.
No one can restrain His hand
Or say to Him, "What have You done?"

At the same time my reason returned to me, and for the glory of my kingdom, my honor and splendor returned to me. My counselors and nobles resorted to me, I was restored to my kingdom, and excellent majesty was added to me. Now I, Nebuchadnezzar, praise and extol and honor the King of heaven, all of whose works *are* truth, and His ways justice. And those who walk in pride He is able to put down.

—Daniel 4:19-37

Readings:

Leadership of any type is a stewardship which means it's temporary. And you're accountable.

—Andy Stanley

The question we have before us is, "How should Christians become involved in politics?" We are asking not "whether" but "how." C. S. Lewis, in one of his writings, is specific about how: Christians in politics should be like serpents and doves. The reference is to Matthew 10:16, where Christ is sending his disciples out into Israel, telling them to be shrewd as serpents and innocent as doves. I think this passage is relevant to politics and journalism as well, especially political journalism. Several years ago a friend pointed this scripture out to me when I asked him where I could find a Biblical guideline to follow as a journalist. Since that time I have tried to follow it, without much success. Few politicians, or journalists for that matter, have succeeded in being both shrewd and innocent. It is easy to be shrewd. It is hard to be innocent. Humility is hard to find in politics and journalism, too. In fact, it is easier to find humility in Washington politics than in Washington journalism these days.

—Fred Barnes

The ultimate measure of a man is not where he stands in the moments of comfort, but where he stands at times of challenge and controversy. Courage faces fear and thereby masters it; cowardice represses fear and is thereby mastered by it. We must constantly build dikes of courage to hold back the flood of fear.

—Martin Luther King, Jr.

Courage is rightly esteemed the first of human qualities because it is the quality which guarantees all others.

—Winston Churchill

Commentary and Questions:

For a half-year or more, depending on how frequently your small group meets, you have been mucking around in politics.

It has almost certainly been a very different season for your small group than any that has gone before it because political conversation, even among Christians, can become hard-edged and passionate. When stakes are high, tempers can be short. Has this happened among your group? Can you recall when and why? If not, is it because you are all like-minded or because you did not seriously wrestle with the issues that divide us as Americans?

Looking forward, are you willing to lead? To do so would require another half-year at least out of your small group routine, a routine that may be comfortable and indeed very useful to your spiritual growth and walk with Christ.

If you are persuaded that politics matter, and that there is a particularly Christian approach to American politics and an agenda of issues that needs attention and movements that need renewal, please consider leaving your group for a season and beginning a new one, using this text again, but bringing together another group of believers you know to run the gauntlet of politics again. Renewing the American Church's understanding of the importance of politics and its commitment to certain crucial ends is a huge undertaking, and it couldn't be accomplished even if a hundred Billy Grahams and a hundred Rick Warrens and a hundred John Paul II's got together at a conference and agreed on a plan of action. It would still require the millions of American Christians who are deeply faithful to move beyond their pews and their church's many committees to activism in the world of politics. That sort of a move will not be sparked by a sermon, no matter how well delivered, because one sermon can only accomplish so much. Nor can a pastor be expected to preach continually or even often on politics. That's not his or her job, though it is a part of his or her job to point to the importance of politics. It is your job because you are a citizen and a Christian in a free society that invites and indeed depends upon your service in politics.

If you have become convinced over the past twenty-six weeks that *anything* needs to be done to improve American politics, then please commit to helping begin that project by bringing together a new group for a defined period of time—twenty-six weeks—and leading the group through this material. Give your group a hiatus and a time certain to return to it, but push out in leadership and try to move others into the activism and commitments necessary to see the vision of Christ's kingdom on earth made more manifest in our country's politics.

Christians do not seek political power to establish a church; at least they ought not to. They don't seek political power for power's sake. But they should seek political influence so that the deepest convictions of Christ's followers—that justice, mercy, and faith be present in increasing amounts on this unredeemed earth— can be achieved as far as possible in these times.

Discuss among yourselves your willingness to start such a study, and who it would be wise to involve. As far as you are comfortable, each one of you should start a group, but if you are not certain of your ability to put together and lead such an effort, work as a twosome.

Finally, ask your pastors what they think of such a project, and if they would be willing to endorse not any particular position or candidate, but a church-wide examination of key issues, perhaps in a recurring forum that doesn't compete with worship or any other church undertaking, but which clearly conveys that the life of the country is important to the life of the church. Expect pastors to be very wary of such an invitation, as there is a long list of troubles that befall politicized congregations, and a prudent pastor will go very slowly toward anything that could divide the flock.

But begin the conversation and seek a way to assure that any undertaking doesn't divide but rather unites people around the commitment that Christ's kingdom on this earth requires government that allows that kingdom to grow unmolested through a vigorous and open expression of Christian faith and the convictions that this faith produces.

Acknowledgements

First off, I use the New King James Version throughout. It has always been my favorite and I hope you'll give it a try.

Charlie Richards was a wonderful partner in this project, one of the rare fellows who understands that Scripture really does speak specifically to the political issues we face today. Charlie is also a superb researcher and writer, and anyone who needs such help should contact me so that I can put you in touch with him.

Dustin Steeve has been an assistant on the radio program throughout his undergraduate years at Biola University, and he and Jennifer Hardy worked to find just the right set of readings for some of the issues discussed herein. My thanks to them both.

Lynne Chapman is now on book number twelve with me, and her abilities only grow greater and her patience deeper. Duane Patterson and Adam Ramsey assure not only the smooth running of the radio show, but also that I need not worry about it at all when I am in a writing rush. These three are the core of the team that makes the program and all related endeavors work, and I am grateful to them.

For the fourteen years I have taught at Chapman University Law School, first Dean Parham Williams and now Dean John Eastman have presided over a young, dynamic, and growing school. They have reflected Chapman University President Jim

Doti's commitment to engaged scholarship in its many forms, including the broadcast variety. The reach of the interviews on my radio show is vast because Chapman University committed to allowing me to engage an audience far beyond the physical classroom, and I am grateful to all three and to a wonderful set of faculty colleagues, many of whom have contributed both on air and off to my thinking.

Barbara Babcock and Gloria Davis have always been ready to help marry the demands of teaching, writing, and journalism. My students have been gracious about sudden departures when an interview became available. I thank them all.

Salem Communications is the home of my radio show, my blog, and the "Hughniverse." Before any other major media company understood the synergy between the radio and the Web, Salem's founders Edward Atsinger and Stuart Epperson had, and they acted on it. The new media infrastructure that has partially liberated American politics from the handicap of a deep left bias which still permeates the now very far fallen titans of old media owes much to these two gentlemen and their colleagues within the management of Salem. David Evans, Greg Anderson, and Joe Davis have led the transition from a radio company to a new media company that includes radio stations, and in so doing have significantly altered the face of American media and continue to do so. Tom Freiling and Eric Jones have been of enormous assistance in taking the radio interviews and converting them into this book and CDs.

I have been especially grateful to Russ Hauth, David Spady, Russ Shubin, and Jonathan Graithwaite, all of whom love politics and public policy as much as I do, and who keep the business of broadcasting focused on the product and its purpose. My colleagues behind microphones, Bill Bennett, Mike Gallagher, Dennis Prager, Michael Medved, Janet Parshall, and Albert Mohler are great friends as well as communicators, and the many other hosts within the Salem network have always been eager to publicize my books even when they did not agree with my points of view. It is an extraordinary company, and people who work within it do so because they view the mission of attracting, informing, and activating America's citizens as crucial to the future of the country. Whether it is Tom Tradup and the Dallas team, a GM in a local market, or a sales staffer making the pitch that keeps us all on the air, Salem's people distinguish it among the media companies scrambling for eyeballs and ears. I especially want to thank those brave souls who regularly sit in behind the microphone for me when I am away: the late Dean Barnett, Jim Geraghty, Carol Platt Liebau, Guy Benson, Mark Larson, Eric Hogue, Michael Steele, and Emmett, the Unblinking Eye. Each sacrifices time and energy in the cause of entertaining yet informative journalism, and I and the audience appreciate them for the effort. Richard Botkin and Bill Lobdell are the friends who stand ready to push me forward when I would rather waste time, and I thank them. John Mark Reynolds and David Allen White are two great thinkers who share all that they have for the glory of God.

As with every other book, the most important person in its completion and success, even as she is to my life, is Betsy, without whom nothing would get done and nothing would be nearly as sweet.

CPSIA information can be obtained
at www.ICGtesting.com
Printed in the USA
FSOW01n1128260417
33578FS

9 781607 913061